Fairway 3

Englisch

Lehrerband

von

Olivia Brandon

Ernst Klett Sprachen Stuttgart

Fairway 3

Englisch

von
Prof. Dr. Herbert Puchta
Jeff Stranks
Peter Lewis-Jones

Lehrerband
von
Olivia Brandon

Beratung
Carol Goodwright, London
Dr. Astrid Krake, München
Eva-Maria Meyer-Dammann, Heidelberg
Helen Paul, Leussow
Julia Shirtliff, Mainz-Kastel
Heidi Staschen, Hamburg
Lynn Strutt, London

1. Auflage 1 6 5 4 3 2 | 2014 13 12 11 10 09

Alle Drucke dieser Auflage können im Unterricht nebeneinander benutzt werden, sie sind untereinander unverändert. Die letzte Zahl bezeichnet das Jahr dieses Druckes.

Internetadresse: http://www.klett.de

Redaktion: David Shallis
Gestaltung: Elmar Feuerbach
Satz: Fotosatz Kaufmann
Druck: Druckerei Ludwig Auer GmbH, Donauwörth
Printed in Germany.

ISBN 3-12-501465-4
ISBN 978-3-12-501465-7

9 783125 014657

Contents

Preface

by Professor Herbert Puchta

'Language learning is a total human experience.'
(Earl Stevick)

Teaching a foreign language successfully is more than transferring information into our learners' brains. It goes beyond the presentation, practice and production of vocabulary and grammar structures, and it is also not just about developing our learners' language skills. As Earl Stevick suggests, there is a wide range of factors that exert a significant influence on the outcomes of the teaching and learning process – language is part of who we are, therefore acquiring a new language is, for many learners a personal and affective experience as much as it is a cognitive process.

If language learning is a total human experience, then the successful teaching of a foreign language requires careful attention to humanistic needs in the language class. Earl Stevick, in fact, stresses that success in a foreign language class depends to a large degree also on 'what goes on inside and between the people in the classroom'. This means that the creation of a supportive learning atmosphere is paramount for teaching a foreign language successfully. Therefore, many teachers in adult education regularly work on the creation of rapport with their learners, and the rapport between the learners in the class. They put a lot of effort into creating a 'can do' atmosphere in their classroom in order to facilitate learners' positive beliefs about their language learning capabilities and to strengthen their self esteem.

The Fairway to learning English

In line with the meaning of the word, the Fairway to learning English for adults offers the teacher a lot of support in facilitating linguistic and cognitive processes while at the same time taking into consideration humanistic aspects of teaching a foreign language to adults. Therefore, in the development of the philosophy and rationale on which Fairway is based, as well as during the creation of the course itself, special emphasis was put on the following principles:

- Learners need clarity
- Learners need practice
- Learners need security
- Learners need success
- Learners need to increase their personal competence

A multi-method approach

In order to address all learner-types efficiently, Fairway follows a 'best practice' approach, including a wide range of methodological applications. Substantial parts of the units follow a solid pattern of **PPP** (presentation, practice and production) and at the same time give the teacher many opportunities to make choices and adapt the teaching to specific classroom situations. In line with the **lexical approach**, the language to be taught has been selected very carefully. With Fairway, learners are exposed to and learn chunks of language, phrases and words that have high frequency value and therefore can easily be transferred to a wide range of uses and contexts. A lot of emphasis is put on the thorough development of reading and listening skills where learners' involvement is secured through the appealing content of the texts on the one hand, and a **task-oriented approach** (as far as pre-, while- and post-reading/listening activities are concerned), on the other.

There is also significant evidence that learners will be better motivated, and learn more successfully, if differences in **learning styles** and learners' **multiple intelligences** are taken into account in the teaching-learning process. The development of a number of activities in Fairway have been influenced by such insights.

The value of human interest based reading
Success in reading and understanding texts in the target language is one of the most important motivational experiences for foreign language learners. Therefore, Fairway puts great emphasis on the development of learners' reading skills and interests. Informative, amusing, appealing and thought-provoking texts are offered both in the classroom sections of the units and in the practice material for home use. Furthermore, the learners are given careful guidance so that they can feel secure in achieving comprehension of the texts in the classroom and at home. All the 'Reading for fun' texts are also recorded on the CD-ROM and therefore offer valuable training in pronunciation.

Introduction

Fairway

Fairway is a 3-level course leading from Level A1 (total beginners) to Level B1 of The Common European Framework of Reference for Languages (CEF).

Fairway 3 covers CEF level B1. On completion of the course, learners can take the TELC B1 Certificate in English exam without additional preparation.

The course components

• Fairway 3: Learner's Book (Lern- und Arbeitsbuch)
with integrated workbook, audio CD and CD-ROM (ISBN: 3-12-501462-X)

• Fairway 3: Teacher's Book
(ISBN: 3-12-501465-4)

The Learner's Book (Lern- und Arbeitsbuch)
Fairway 3 is a course book and practice book in one, and consists of 14 units, plus an introductory Welcome unit and a short closing unit called See You! The 14 main units are divided into A and B sections, each providing work for at least one 90-minute session. Each of the classroom sections is followed by a Practice section, which can be used for homework or classroom work, as required. There are also five Self-check units, one after every third unit. The final unit is followed by a checklist of Level B1 descriptors, which learners can use to evaluate the progress they have made during the course.

Packaged with the student's book are an audio CD and a hybrid CD/CD-ROM which contain all the listening material in the Learner's Book. The CD/CD-ROM contains the Reading for Fun texts (tapescripts and recordings), plus the complete vocabulary in word and sound (see Reading texts).

For further information concerning the CEF, visit the Council of Europe web-site:
http://culture2.coe.int/portfolio/inc.asp?L=E&M=$t/208-1-0-1/documents_intro/common_framework.html

For information concerning Portfolio models, visit the Council of Europe web-site:
http://www.coe.int/T/DG4/Portfolio/?L=E&M=/main_pages/portfolios.html

For further information concerning the B1 examination, visit the TELC web-site:
http://www.sprachenz.de/

Introduction

The units

Each unit directly reflects the three-fold philosophy of the book: clarity, security and success. Each of the 14 main units is divided into an A and B section. The classroom section of the unit (white pages) begins with revision work which also points the way to the subject matter of the section ahead. This is followed by an activity that introduces language to be worked on in detail. There are usually four to six steps of varying length and complexity in each section. The concluding task in each section, usually in the form of a group activity, incorporates all the material presented in the section. In this task-oriented step learners work with the material in a personalised context.

The clear structure of the unit is further enhanced through a system of coloured boxes and language bubbles.

- Speech bubbles
  indicate the language area.
- Blue boxes
  present the grammar in table form.
- White boxes
  contain language prompts. This is the language to be used in the tasks.
- Beige boxes
  present additional information of varying types. The TIPP box, which is mainly in German in Fairway 3, includes a number of learning strategies, as well as some suggestions for successful communication. The Memo box clarifies language points or gives additional language input. My vocab box serves as a gathering point for personal vocabulary.

The Practice sections

The Practice section (beige pages) directly follows the classroom section. This section contains no new grammar. Each Practice section concludes with an authentic Reading for Fun text which can be listened to and read on the CD-ROM. The purpose of these texts is to arouse interest in the topics, give pleasure to the learners and instil in them a sense of accomplishment and success.

The Self-checks

The Self-checks (green pages) are to be found after every third unit and enable learners to check their own progress. Each Self-check is presented in multiple-choice format, lending it a test character and setting it distinctly apart from the Practice sections. The first section of the Self-check is identical in format to the TELC B1 Certificate in English exam, which can be taken upon completion of Fairway 3. The second section, *Die wichtigsten Wendungen*, tests the main grammatical structures that learners have been working on. In the third section, *Mein Lernfortschritt*, learners tick the things they feel they can now do in English. These items are all CEF B1 descriptors.

In the Self-checks learners may occasionally be confronted with unfamiliar vocabulary. They need to develop their own strategies for dealing with this situation as it may also occur in the exam.

The Checklist for Level B1

The CEF B1 descriptors for communicative competence are listed in the Checklist Level B1 on pp. 163 – 164 (blue pages). Here, learners can realistically evaluate their progress thus far. This will help them to articulate future learning goals.

The Appendix

Info gap activities: Input for Learner B
Grammar
Keys to Practice sections and Self-checks
Tapescripts (those not included in the units)
Unit vocabulary
Alphabetical wordlist
CD Tracks (timing)
Instructions for using the CD-ROM

The audio CD and CD-ROM

The Learner's Book comes with two free CDs. These contain recordings of all the texts and other activities which are marked with a blue track number, e.g. CD 1/1. CD 1 is a hybrid which also contains the CD-ROM. This is an integral part of the course and has three major components:

1. An alphabetical vocabulary
   Learners can use this if they simply want to hear how a word is pronounced. It can be accessed immediately via the ABC-symbol in the mask.
2. A unit vocabulary
   Here learners can listen to (loudspeaker symbol) and repeat (red circle/white square) vocabulary. A German translation of each word is also available (glasses symbol).
3. Reading for Fun
   These texts are listed according to unit. Learners can read and listen to the text and the speed of the recording can be adjusted to meet individual needs.

The Teacher's Book (Lehrerband)

This provides step-by-step teaching notes for every unit in the Learner's Book. Each unit starts with a summary of the learning targets for that unit, and each section of the unit is preceded by a detailed overview of the new language that learners will be dealing with.

The teaching notes include:
- keys to the exercises;
- tapescripts as necessary;
- extra information on particular language points;
- suggestions for further practice;
- photocopiable materials, to be used as handouts and/or overhead OHP transparencies.

Symbols used in the Teacher's Book

CD 1/1	Track number
➡	Extra information
⚠	Caution!

Teaching with Fairway 3

In general
Before planning a lesson, look at the grey boxes at the beginning of the teaching notes for the relevant unit. These show the language involved at a glance, together with extras that you might want to bring to the lesson and the photocopiable materials you could use.

The teaching notes that follow take you through the unit step by step and include tapescripts and keys for all the activities. Use the photocopiable materials and extra activities described in the teaching notes to give your learners further practice as necessary.

Essential classroom equipment
Board or flip chart
CD player

An overhead projector (OHP) will also be useful, if available.

Pairwork and group work
Fairway 3 implements the task-oriented approach, which means that learners are frequently asked to work in pairs or groups. This will give them more confidence in their spoken language skills and more opportunity to experiment than when working alone or as part of a large class. In addition, they will have an opportunity to bring their own ideas and interests into the class.

The level of authenticity in the pair or group tasks is decisive for the effectiveness of group or pair work. It is important that learners approach each task with a view toward personalising the work. Very often key language is presented as a prompt for the learners. It would be all too easy to simply fill in words here. This, however, would be defeating the purpose. Learners are invited to give each task some thought, then bring themselves in personally. The language in the prompt boxes provides the skeleton which can truly be brought to life by the learners' enthusiasm and motivation.

It is important that learners do not always work in the same group or with the same partner. An occasional change means that learners profit from the knowledge of different learners. Group work activities also provide an opportunity for the teacher to go round and give individual help and stimulus.

Learning and storing vocabulary
Vocabulary acquisition is, perhaps, the most important single aspect of language learning. Without vocabulary, ideas cannot be expressed.

In Fairway 3 vocabulary is presented in a variety of ways. In general, the meaning of new words will be more or less clear from the context in which they occur. Learners are also asked to guess meanings, match words with pictures, find opposites or cognates, complete the spelling of new words, find the new words in texts, and much more.

Personalising vocabulary is an important aspect of language learning. Through the use of 'My vocab' boxes learners are encouraged to personalise vocabulary and record additional words they would like to learn.

Learners are also encouraged to learn new words in context, or group them in word families or word fields, as this aids memory. Word maps are used in several units to help learners organise vocabulary into manageable word fields. Word maps have the additional advantage that they can grow as vocabulary is expanded.

Vocabulary acquisition outside the classroom is also an essential aspect of successful learning. Here are a few ideas you might like to discuss with the learners:

Learners can write new words on small cards that can be kept in the pocket for practice outside the classroom, for example, in the train on the way to work. Words can also be written on individual cards or pieces of paper and placed at strategic points in the home (e.g. kitchen, bathroom).

Learners can note the use of English words around them in many aspects of daily life: in advertisements; on product descriptions; on radio or TV; in newspapers; in travel catalogues, on the Internet, etc.

They can practise vocabulary by talking to themselves. When walking down the street one can identify what one observes in the target language, e.g. *That's a green car.*

It is important that learners come to realise that there is a multitude of ways to effectively acquire and store vocabulary and that everyone has an enormous creative potential for doing this. Vocabulary acquisition can be exciting and fun. It is important to get this message across to the learner.

Working with dialogues

Dialogues are very much at the heart of Fairway 3. Much of the new language material is presented via the dialogue. While having all the advantages of a reading text, the dialogue has the additional advantage that it can be worked with in a far greater variety of ways than a simple reading text ever could be.

The dialogues are presented in a wide variety of ways. Some of them are complete. Others are jumbled and learners must put them in the correct order. In some cases, learners listen and fill in information which is missing in the dialogue text. In other cases, words from a list have to be written into the text. Still other dialogues serve as information for completing a task based on a reading text.

No matter how they are presented, all the dialogues are recorded on the CD. As the dialogues are of varying length and complexity, it will be necessary to present the recording accordingly. In some cases, learners will need to hear the recording several times. Judicious use of the pause button at the end of a line or sentence can also be very helpful with complex texts or weaker groups.

Just as there is a great diversity of texts, there is also a wide range of effective ways to work with them. Suggestions for working with each dialogue are made in the teaching notes.

Working with recordings

1. In general, learners should simply listen to the recording the first time through, and not read along. Ask them to either close their books or cover the dialogue with a piece of paper. This will help them to prepare for the authentic, real world situation, where there will be no written text to follow.
2. Learners listen and read the dialogue silently along with the recording.
3. Learners mumble the tapescript along with the recording. This may seem an odd idea but it gives them a chance to get their tongues around new sounds before they have to 'perform' in front of other learners.
4. Play the recording and stop at the end of each line. The whole class repeats the line in chorus. Many learners value the opportunity to practise as a group before risking a solo performance. (See the next section on 'Choral Drilling' for more information on this type of practice.)
5. Learners close their books. Write the dialogue on the board. Let two learners read the dialogue aloud and then erase some of the words before asking two more learners to read it again. Carry on erasing, leaving only key words. You will often find that you can erase the entire dialogue and learners will still be able to perform it. This practice helps train memory in a challenging fashion which learners actually enjoy once they are accustomed to it. The dialogue which lends itself particularly well to this type of practice is the short situational dialogue that learners encounter again and again, such as a shopping dialogue or restaurant dialogue.
6. Ask learners to act out the dialogue and express different types of emotion, such as enthusiasm, anger, boredom, etc.
7. Learners personalise the dialogue by replacing certain words with items of their own.
8. Learners listen to a dialogue with books closed. Ask them to call out any key words they understood. Gather them on the board, then ask learners to help sort the mosaic of words into the proper order. Slowly work toward the skeleton dialogue before playing the recording again.
9. In advance, write individual key words of a dialogue on cards, including a few distractors. Ask learners to gather round in a group, then lay the cards out on a table so that everyone can see them. Play the recording and learners take a card when they have understood a word. They then work together using their words to re-construct the skeleton dialogue.

Choral drilling

There are many sub-steps in Fairway 3 that require learners to listen and repeat. Practising the pronunciation of words and phrases is an essential part of language acquisition and has beneficial effects not only on learner's oral output but also on their listening skills. To work effectively with oral drilling, the teacher needs a well-developed system.

The first thing is to recognise that the problems being dealt with in pronunciation are mechanical. Learners need physical practice in getting their lips and tongues around English sounds, both in isolation and in connected speech. The aim is 'fluidity'. Pronunciation is like aerobics for the mouth, and should be handled as such. There are many ways to conduct a choral drill efficiently, and make it fun. In the end you will develop your own style, but to help you get started, here are some basic principles worth following:

1. Start organised choral drilling from Day 1 and do it regularly (every lesson).
2. Be strict when it comes to choral drilling. All attention must be on you as the leader of the activity (but making it feel like fun will help!).
3. Never do choral drilling of an unknown language item! The meaning must always be clear before you focus on the form.
4. Always model the item first, making sure that learners just listen. Model the item three times, making sure it is always the same. And try to keep a reasonable speed in the model.
5. Use your hand to beat the rhythm of the sentence (and if necessary to show the intonation pattern), like an orchestra conductor. Imagine that learners can read the word or sentence floating in front of you. This means that it starts on your right and runs to your left. Beat the rhythm in that direction. The beating should be silent: any sound, such as clapping your hands, disturbs the clarity of the model you are giving.
6. Now it is the learners' turn. Use the hand movements (right to left) to 'conduct' the learners in chorus. Don't tolerate any sloppiness here. Get them (all of them) to chorus the word or sentence three times in unison. During this stage, remain silent so that you can actually hear what learners are saying.
7. Go swiftly round the class and use your hand to conduct each learner in a quick single solo drill, dealing with individual problems where necessary. Don't accept shyness here.

This may seem a very 'teacherish' and time-consuming undertaking at first, but once you have developed confidence in your own style of organised drilling, and have trained your learners to 'jump through the hoops' at your command, you will find that it is possible to focus effectively on the pronunciation of even a long model sentence in less than 60 seconds, during which time each learner will have said the sentence altogether four times (three times in chorus and once individually). Your learners will very quickly recognize the value to themselves, and will cooperate fully.

Presenting language

In Fairway 3, grammar input is restricted to what is essential for communication in everyday situations. New tenses in Fairway 3 include the Past Perfect and the passive tenses.

In the main, new language is presented inductively or by 'guided discovery'. This means that the teacher can often work through the steps and simply let the book do the teaching. The new grammar, which appears in the blue Grammar box, sums up the grammar point being taught and calls learners' attention to what they have been using throughout the step. A deductive presentation of the grammar is seldom necessary.

The presentation of the Past perfect tense, Unit 8B, pp. 89 – 91, may serve to illustrate the point:

1c)

Learners complete a dialogue by adding the missing words/phrases from the recording. Each contains a verb in the Past perfect.

2a)

Learners listen to the recording and correct sentences.

2b)

Learners complete the written dialogue by filling in phrases from a list.

2c)

Listen and check. Learners again hear the Present perfect verbs in context while reading the text.

2d)

The grammar structure is presented in the Grammar box with examples from the dialogue. Learners deduce the rule, then complete it in German.

3a)

In a pair activity, learners personalise the language in a very controlled context.

3b)

Matching sentence halves with a partner. (Past simple and Past perfect).

4a)

Listening activity. Story about a memorable weekend. Learners put pictures in the correct order.

4b)

Learners listen and check their work.

4c)

Learners answer a question about the content of the story.

4d)

Listening activity. Learners choose the correct option.

4e)

Pair activity. Learners retell the story using the Past simple and Past perfect tenses.

5a + 5b)

Learners personalise the language material and talk to a partner about a particularly memorable weekend they have had.

It will be clear from this representation that new grammar structures receive very thorough practice in context and require almost no presentation in the traditional manner. The blue Grammar boxes simply sum up the work done through the steps.

List of functions

Unit 5A
—

Unit 5B
Expressing dislike: *I don't really like ...*

Unit 6A
—

Unit 6B
Expressing displeasure: *Stop it, Bill!*
Criticising: *Don't be silly, Jenny.*
Expressing disinterest: *Who cares about ...?*
Giving the source of some information: *According to (the forecast), ...*

Unit 7A
Expressing degrees of certainty: *We'll probably go to Europe ...; I probably won't ever ...; I might get to see (Paris); I'll definitely (plant a tree).*
Retracting a statement: *No, that's a lie.*
Recommending something: *You should go; That's really something you should try and see.*
Expressing hopes: *I hope to see ...; I'd love to ... one day.*
Expressing regret: *Unfortunately not.*
Making excuses: *The problem's time; Life's too short.*
Encouraging someone to do something: *So do it.*
Keeping options open: *We haven't made any definite plans yet, but ...*

Unit 7B
Expressing surprise: *I can hardly believe (I'm leaving on Friday).*
Expressing regret: *It's a pity ...; Yes, it's a shame.*
Asking for a suggestion: *What would you like to do today?*
Suggesting: *What do you suggest?; I know! (Capilano!)*
Declining: *Oh no. I don't think so, thanks; I wouldn't (walk over that bridge) if you paid me.*
Persuading: *We could just (go and look); Oh, come on! You're usually so adventurous.*

Unit 8A
Commenting on someone's mood: *What are you so happy about?; You're in a good mood; What's the matter with you?; What are you so bothered about?*
Expressing pleasure: *That's great news; Fantastic.*
Congratulating someone: *Congratulations!; She really deserves it; Good for her; Well done.*
Expressing sympathy: *Sorry to hear that.*
Wishing someone well: I'm sure you'll do better next time; Better luck next time.
Expressing disappointment: *That's easy for you to say; I think I could have done better.*
Calming someone: *Calm down!; Don't get so angry about it; Take it easy.*

Unit 8B
Expressing regret: *I'm ringing to say sorry (that I didn't go to your party).*
Making excuses: *I wanted to go but (I felt really ill).*
Asking for information: *What was wrong?; Anyway, tell me, how was (the party)?; Why was that?*
Expressing hope: *Maybe next time.*

Unit 9A
Asking for a recommendation: *Can you recommend one?*
Asking for permission: *May I have a look at ...?*
Asking for information: *What do I need to know about it?; Does it come with ...?*
Explaining something: *That refers to (the quality); It means you can (take about 32 pictures).*
Asking for confirmation: *So you really would recommend ...?*

Confirming: *For the price, you can't buy better.*
Expressing surprise: *What! It doesn't (come with a case)?*
Accepting a situation: *Well, I suppose I'll have to (buy one of them).*
Giving permission: *Feel free …; Go ahead, it's all yours; Certainly, help yourself; Please do.*

Unit 9B
Telephoning:
- Offering assistance: *How may I help you?*
- Putting someone through: *Would you hold the line, please?; Can you hang on a moment? I'll see if he's around.*
- Saying someone is not available: *I'm afraid her extension is engaged at the moment; Sorry, he's not here.*
- Offering to take a message: *Would you like to/Do you want to leave a message?*
- Saying you'll call back: *I'll call again this afternoon; I'll ring later on.*

Saying goodbye (informally): *Cheers.*
Agreeing: *I completely agree with the point that …*
Disagreeing: *I'm not sure I agree with the idea that …; I don't agree at all with the writer when she says …; I think …*

Unit 10A
Making suggestions/recommendations: *Shall we (stop and have lunch)?; We should ask the waiter; You really ought to go to …; You shouldn't forget to visit (the cathedral).*
Agreeing: *Anywhere is fine with me.*
Expressing relief: *I thought you'd never ask.*
Estimating: *It shouldn't (take you more than 20 minutes).*
Interrupting someone: *Excuse me for intruding but …*

Unit 10B
Apologising: *Oh, sorry. My mistake,*
Expressing enthusiasm: *Great! I can hardly wait to (see the paintings).*
Expressing surprise: *But hold on …*
Expressing disbelief: *I mean, come on!*
Making a suggestion: *I think we'd better (have a guide), don't you?*

Unit 11A
Complaining: *I'm not very happy with …*
Expressing regret: *I'm sorry to hear that; That's a shame, sir; I'm sorry you think that, sir.*
Asking for details: *What exactly is the problem?*
Playing for time: *Let me see.*
Responding to a complaint: *I'm afraid I can't really help you. The man you need to talk to is …*
Expressing dissatisfaction: *Well, that's no good; That's exactly what I'm afraid of; You really don't seem very interested in helping me at all.*
Countering: *Well, I do.*

Unit 11B
Asking about probability: *Do you think you'll (go out for a meal this weekend)?; What's the chance of (you going out for a meal this weekend)?; How likely (are you to go out for a meal this weekend)?*
Expressing probability: *I might; There's a small chance I might; It's difficult to say because …*

Unit 12A
Explaining what you need: *I need one of those things to …; Have you got one of those things for …*

Unit 12B
—

Unit 13A
Responding to a suggestion: *I could give it a go, I suppose.*

Unit 13B
Expressing opinions: *I really like the way the story …; I thought (the story) was a bit silly because …; The only part I didn't think was so good was …; What I liked most about the story was …; I wasn't really convinced by the …*
Agreeing: I agree with most of what you say but …; That's exactly what I feel, too.
Disagreeing: I don't really agree with anything you say; I take your point, but I'm afraid I don't agree completely.

Unit 14A
—

Unit 14B
—

See you!
Suggesting: *We must keep in touch.*
Expressing an intention: *I'll phone you.*
Wishing someone well: *The best of luck; I'd like to wish you all the best; Look after yourself.*
Greeting: *Give my regards to …*

Welcome

Unit summary

This unit gives learners who have worked together previously with Fairway 1 and Fairway 2 the opportunity to greet one another and get to know any newcomers to the course.

Have we met before?

Focus

Introductions

Greeting people one hasn't seen for a while

Interview activity focusing on question forms

Learning strategies

Functions

Greeting: *I haven't seen you for ages. What have you been up to?; Have we met before?*

Grammar

Revision of question forms

What you need

Welcome 1b): A small soft ball; one copy of p. 108 for each pair of learners in the class.

Welcome 1f): Some pleasant background music; sticky notes to be used as name tags.

Welcome 2: One photocopy of p. 109 for each learner.

Welcome 4a): One photocopy of p. 110 for each pair of learners.

Welcome 4d): (Additional activity 1) One photocopy of p. 111 for each group of three learners.

Starting the course

If there are new learners in the group, introduce yourself, using the short form of the verb and your first name.

If you have brought a soft ball to the lesson, introduce yourself and add something that you like, e.g. *I'm (Anna) and I like (swimming)*, then throw the ball to one of the learners. This person introduces him/herself, then throws the ball to another participant. Carry on until all the learners have introduced themselves.

Suggest that learners use first names during the course as this is usual in English-speaking countries, especially in informal situations. Using first names in class also helps to create a relaxed and pleasant working atmosphere.

Learners will introduce themselves and find out more about each other later in the lesson. They will feel more at ease if they know the names of unfamiliar participants before work begins.

1a)

Ask learners to look at the picture and describe the situation. Where are the women? What is the occasion? Do they know each other already or are they meeting for the first time?

Play the two dialogues and learners decide which one goes with the picture.

CD 1/1

Dialogue 1

□ Hello. I haven't seen you for ages. How are you?
○ Fine, thanks. And you?
□ Me too. So, what have you been up to?
○ Not a lot. Well, I went on holiday to Italy.
□ Wonderful! Was it good?
○ It was great. We had a fantastic time.

Dialogue 2

△ Have we met before?
▼ I don't think so. I'm Natasha, I'm a friend of Michael's.
△ Hi, Natasha, my name's Sonia. Nice to meet you.
▼ Nice to meet you, too. Do you know many people here?
△ No, I don't. Do you know anyone?
▼ Yes, one or two people. Let me introduce you to them.

1a) Key

Learners' own answers

1b)

Make one photocopy of p. 108 for each pair of learners in the class. Cut up the dialogues and give one set to each pair. Learners arrange the two dialogues in the correct order, then number the lines in their books.

1b) Key

See the tapescript in 1a) above.

Dialogue 1:
5, 1, 3, 2, 6, 4

Dialogue 2:
6. 5, 2, 3, 1, 4

1c)

Play the recording again so that learners can check their work. Tell them to leave the dialogues laid out, as they will need them in step 1e) when they practise the dialogue in pairs.

1d)

Learners now work individually and match the German translations with English phrases from the dialogues.

1d) Key

1. Was hast du so gemacht?
2. Kennen wir uns?
3. Schön, Sie kennen zu lernen.
4. Danke, gut.
5. ewig
6. nicht sehr viel

1e)

Learners now practise the dialogues in pairs. Tell them to use their own names when practising the second dialogue. Remind them to practise both roles in each of the dialogues.

1f)

Learners now get up and walk around, greeting people they already know and introducing themselves to those they don't know. They should speak to as many people as possible in the time allotted.

Play some pleasant background music while they do this. Let them continue until they have had time to speak to a number of other participants.

When they have returned to their seats, give each learner a sticky ('Post-it') note . Ask them to write their name on it and attach it to their clothing. Although they have just spoken with each other they may not be able to remember everyone's names. The name tags will also be useful for the next task.

2

This step is in two parts. First, learners revise question forms that were presented and practised in Fairway 1 and 2. Ask them to look at no. 1, then write questions for nos. 2 – 7. The first words of the questions have been given, to simplify the task. Check by asking various learners to read out their questions.

Learners now walk around interviewing other people in the class and noting their responses. To make this easier, give each learner a photocopy of the interview sheet on p. 109. Note that the first words of the questions are also given on the sheet.

Don't rush this activity! Set a time-limit, but allow long enough for learners to interview two other people. When the time is up, ask each person to report one interesting thing they found out about another learner.

2 Key

1. Where are you from?
2. Have you got a car?
3. Do you smoke?
4. Do you speak more than one language?
5. Do you prefer theatre to cinema?
6. Were you in this class last semester?
7. Did you travel somewhere last year?
8. How long have you learned English?

3a)

Ask learners to look at the pictures of Nora and André and speculate about their ages, nationalities and reasons for learning English. Then play the recording, pausing between the two descriptions to allow learners to fill in the missing information. If necessary, play the recording a second time.

CD 1/2

See the tapescripts on p. 187 of the Learner's Book.

3a) Key

Nora:
Nationality: Italian
Age: 22
Reasons for learning English: She wants to speak better. She needs it for a future job.

André:
Nationality: French
Age: 67
Reasons for learning English: He wanted a new hobby and he likes to travel.

3b)

Learners now work in groups of four and discuss their reasons for learning English. When the group activity has ended, ask learners to give feedback from their groups and gather some of the reasons on the board.

4a)

In the closing unit of Fairway 2 ('See you' p. 163, Step 6a), learners were given some ideas about how they could keep up their English during a longer break. They ticked the ideas that seemed relevant and useful for them personally.

In this activity learners discuss how they actually worked with English during the break. As most learners will not have Fairway 2 with them, make one copy of p. 110 for each pair of learners in the class. Cut them in two and hand them out. Ask learners to read through them and tick the ones that they tried out during the break. Those new to Fairway can simply tick the suggestions they have tried themselves at some point or think might be useful for them in future.

When everyone has finished, discuss this as with the whole class and find out which activities were most popular and whether learners felt they profited from this work.

4b)

The list of learning strategies presented in this activity expands on the ideas presented in Fairway 2 (see 4a). Learners now work individually, reading the list and evaluating the suggestions as they feel appropriate.

4c)

Learners continue to work individually and add their own ideas to the list. Walk around during this phase and help learners with any new vocabulary.

Some more possibilities:
Talk to yourself in English.
Re-write dialogues from the text using different information.
Keep a learner's diary in English.

4d)

Learners now work in groups of three or four and compare their answers. They could make a statistic of the most popular ideas and those that are least popular. They first compare their answers, then write down the one or two ideas that were most popular with their group and one idea which no one seemed to like. Ask each group to present their results.

Additional Activity 1: Spin the pen
This game revises grammar and vocabulary presented in Fairway 1 and 2. Make a copy of the game sheet on p. 111 for each group of three.

Rules:
Tell learners to put a pen in the middle of the wheel. Explain that they should take turns to spin the pen and all three of them must answer the questions or talk about the topic the pen points to.

If the pen points to a question/topic learners have already dealt with, they should spin the pen again until it points to a new question/topic.

The game finishes when all the learners have answered every question.

Additional Activity 2: What's new in Fairway 3?
This activity could be used to introduce the book to new participants in the course and show those learners returning to the course that the method and book set-up have not changed in Fairway 3. Tell learners they have five minutes to go through the book and write down all the features they can find, such as Grammar boxes, the 'Reading for Fun' texts, etc. Then ask new course members to call out a feature they have on their list. A participant from the previous course should explain this feature. Their contributions can then be amplified by other learners or by you.

Two participants from the previous course could work together and look for new and interesting aspects in Fairway 3, such as more reading texts, thought-provoking visuals, cartoons, etc. Ask each pair to choose the unit that looks most interesting, then comment briefly on their choice.

Features that should be mentioned:

Grammar boxes (blue)
Memo boxes (beige)
My vocab boxes (beige)
TIPP boxes (beige)
The Practice section (beige pages)
Reading for Fun texts (at the end of Practice sections)
Self-checks (after every three units)
Grammar section
Keys to Practice sections and Self-checks
Tapescripts
Unit vocabulary
Alphabetical wordlist
Information on inside front cover
Information on back flap

Companies with a tradition

Unit summary

The first part of this unit focuses on a variety of jobs and the personal skills and characteristics needed to do them well. The second part of the unit features two Irish companies with a long tradition: Tullamore Dew and Waterford Crystal. Grammar focus is on the verbs *need to/have to*. The Present perfect simple and the Present perfect progressive are also revised, practised and contrasted with each other. Learners write a job description and also prepare and give a one-minute presentation on a topic of their choice.

Part A: You need to be interested

Focus

Professions

Skills and personal characteristics required for particular jobs

Written description of one's own job or a dream job

Functions

Agreeing/disagreeing: *I agree.; I don't.*

Expressing uncertainty: *I'm not sure.*

Expressing opinions: *I think …; He definitely needs to be …*

Grammar

have to/don't have to (Revision)

need to/don't need to

What you need

Unit 1A, 1a): Photocopies of p. 112, as required.

Unit 1A, 4d): At least one dictionary for group use.

1a) Revision: professions

This activity revises professions and the language used when speculating about something. Ask learners to look at the list of professions (below the instructions). Pronounce each word and elicit the meaning from the learners.

Then ask them to look at the names on the right. Pronounce each of the names as one would in English. Ignore the two photos for the moment.

➡ Sinead

This Irish (woman's) name is pronounced / sɪnˈeɪd /.

Learners now work individually and match the professions with the names. If they aren't certain, they should guess. They should use the phrases in the box when reporting back to you.

For more information about the eight people, see the photocopiable sheet on p. 112. You might like to cut this up, separating the names and the biographical details, and ask learners to match them.

1a) Key

Anna Pavlova – dancer
Liam Neeson – actor
Oscar Niemeyer – architect
Sinead O'Connor – singer
Florence Nightingale – nurse
Oscar Wilde – writer
Hillary Clinton – politician
Donald Trump – businessman

1b)

Ask the group to speculate about which of the people in 1a) are from Ireland.

1b) Key

Liam Neeson
Sinead O'Connor
Oscar Wilde

1c)

Learners now work in groups of three or four. Tell them they have two minutes to list as many famous Irish men and women as they can. When the time is up, find out which group has the most names on their list and ask them to read them out. Gather them on the board, then call for additions from other groups' lists.

Some names that might be mentioned:

William Butler Yeats (1865-1939)
Poet, dramatist, mystic and public figure. He received the Nobel Prize for Literature in 1923. He was one of the driving forces behind the Irish Literary Revival and was co-founder of the Abbey Theatre.

James Joyce (1882-1941)
Expatriate Irish writer and poet. He is considered by many to be the most influential writer of the 20th century. He is best known for his novels *Ulysses* and *Finnegan's Wake*, as well as for his short story collection *The Dubliners*.

St. Patrick (c. 385-461)
Apostle of Ireland. He was a missionary in Ireland and travelled widely among the chiefs. He fixed his see at Armagh. The only literary remains of the saint are his *Confessions* and a letter addressed to a British chieftain.

Jonathan Swift (1667-1745)
Clergyman and political journalist. He is best-known for his scathing satire. His most famous work is certainly *Gulliver's Travels*.

2

Ask learners to cover the bottom half of the page with a piece of paper. Then ask them to read the speech bubble and the three statements; elicit the meaning of each. Make certain that the meaning of each one is clear. At this point you needn't offer explanations regarding the participial *-ing* form in the statements, e.g. *businesswoman working in Ireland, researcher on a working visit.*

Play the recording and learners mark their answers. If necessary, play the recording a second time.

CD 1/3
See the tapescript on p. 187 of the Learner's Book.

2 Key
3. The customer is an Austrian researcher on a working visit.

3a)

Ask learners to look again at the statement in the speech bubble. Then ask them to close their books. Explain the activity. Tell them they are going to hear a continuation of the dialogue they have just heard. They are to listen to the recording and make notes while listening.

Before playing the recording, discuss good note-taking strategy. In this case, it would be helpful to speculate about the type of information that might be forthcoming, e.g. the topics the two women might mention. When listening, which kinds of information should one listen for? (important key words, e.g. nouns and verbs).

Make sure learners understand that they are not expected to note down everything of importance, and that this is not the goal of the activity. The aim is to piece the dialogue together as a group, using bits of information that various individuals have gleaned from the recording. Mention, as well, that they shouldn't fret if they lose the thread of the dialogue. If this happens, they should just pick up where they can. Others in the group might be able to fill in the points they missed.

Play the recording once and learners make their notes. Ask various learners to call out one bit of information they noted down. Gather them on the board, then put the pieces of the puzzle together (orally) as completely as possible. The result may be quite patchy and incomplete, but there will certainly be enough information so that everyone understands the gist of the dialogue.

CD 1/4
See the dialogue in 3b).

3b)

Ask learners to open their books, then play the recording again while they read the text. Working individually, learners mark the statements true or false. They should underline the statements in the text which confirm their choices.

3b) Key
True: 1, 3, 4
False: 2, 5

3c)

Before learners set out to practise the dialogue with a partner, ask them to read the text again and mark any words or phrases that are still unclear. Ask them to call these out and elicit the meanings from other learners. Learners then practise the dialogue in pairs.

3d)

This activity focuses on collocations. Working individually, learners match the halves. They can check back with the dialogue text if they are uncertain.

3d) Key
1c, 2a, 3e, 4d, 5b

1. I work under a lot of pressure.
2. I'm responsible for Ireland and the UK.
3. I've got to meet deadlines.
4. My job keeps me busy all day.
5. I'm in the travel industry.

4a)

Learners have already listened to the recording several times, read it and practised it with a partner, so it should be easy for them to complete this task without referring back to the text. Learners work individually and tick the correct boxes.

Ask learners to look at the Grammar box. Check that the difference between *have to and need to is clear by asking them to personalize the examples in the box.*

Also elicit the question form using *have to*, e.g. *Do you have to ...?*, which follows the same pattern as *Do you need to ...?* Both of these verbs are extremely useful, as the dialogue text illustrates. Ask learners to read through the dialogue text once more and underline all the examples of phrases using these verbs.

4a) Key
A guide needs ...

to set up meetings
to have a lot of energy
to be very patient all the time
to be interested in people and places

4b)

This activity focuses on more jobs. Pronounce each of the words and ask learners to repeat. Then they work individually and tick the characteristics they think are important for the various jobs.

4c)

Learners now work in small groups and talk about their opinions, using the language in the box.

Before they begin the activity, focus on the language in the prompt box. Ask if they can think of other ways of expressing opinions and gather these on the board. Some possibilities: *I think ...; You're right*. You might like to introduce the softener *I'm sorry, ... (I'm sorry, I don't; I'm sorry, but I don't agree) since* a simple *I don't* could sound rather curt, depending on the speaker's intonation.

4d)

Learners now personalise the language they have been working with. Each learner thinks of a job he/she knows well. Then, working individually, they write a few sentences about it, using the verbs *need to/have to*. They can refer back to the dialogue for ideas and use a dictionary if necessary. Walk around the class during the writing phase, helping with any new words.

4e)

When learners have finished their sentences, they work in small groups again. Each person reads out the sentences they have written and the others in the group try to guess the job.

5a)

In this listening task learners listen and mark the correct option in each of the sentences. First ask learners to read the statements. Elicit the meaning of the various choices before playing the recording. They should try to underline the answers as they listen. To diminish stress, you could use the pause button at a couple of strategic points in the text and give learners a moment to mark their answer before continuing. If necessary play the recording a second time.

CD 1/5

See the tapescript on p. 187 of the Learner's Book.

5a) Key

1. He is a stockbroker.
2. He works in finance.
3. He works for a bank.
4. He works twelve hours a day.
5. He often works at the weekend.
6. He works on his own.
7. He loves his job.
8. Joan is worried about him.

5b)

Now ask learners to read the two questions. Play the recording once more and learners listen for the answers.

Ask learners to look at the sentences in 5a) again, read them and underline all the collocations with the verb *work*, i.e. *work in, work for, work at, work on (your) own*. Suggest that learners create special places (separate sheets of paper, for example) where important verbs can be collected and expanded upon as need be.

5b) Key

1. It's a very important job.
2. She worries because he works too much and hasn't got a girlfriend.

5c)

Now learners write a text about their own job or their dream job. This needs to be handled sensitively, as some people in your class may be unemployed. Point out that they can write about a dream job, a job they may have once done, or a job someone else does. The description should include some information about the job and cover the characteristics the person should possess in order to meet the demands of the job.

Rather than doing this in their books, learners could write their texts on a piece of paper which you can collect for correction when everyone has finished. This would give you a good idea about their writing ability, especially of those new to the class. Return the descriptions in the next session and focus on mistakes that came up several times. Avoid mentioning names, however! Correction is best carried out in the form of general feedback.

You also might like to suggest that learners put this text into their Portfolio if they are pleased with their text. This would offer suitable documentation of their writing skills at this point in their learning. For more information concerning the Language Portfolio, see the Introduction, p. 5.

Part B: The company's been growing ...

Focus
History of Tullamore Dew and Waterford Crystal
Numbers: Rounding up and down
Mini-presentations on a personal topic

Functions
Agreeing: *Me, too.*

Grammar
Present perfect simple vs. Present perfect progressive (Revision)

Pronunciation
Sounds: /□/ ('schwa') as in *ov<u>er</u>*
Linking words

1a) Revision: *need*

This step revises the qualities needed for specific jobs. Here the central figure is a tour guide.

Ask learners to look at the list. Read the phrases in the list and ask learners to repeat after you. Check the pronunciation (particularly with words like *humour, creative, patient, pressure*). Which of the qualities do learners think would be important for a tour guide at the Tullamore Dew Heritage Centre?

1a) Key
Learners' own opinions

1b)

Learners now work in groups of three and exchange opinions using the language in the box.

2a)

Ask learners to close their books. Tell them their next task involves reading a short introductory text about the Heritage Centre. Ask them to work in pairs and think of one question that might be answered in the text, then read it out to the class.

Now ask learners to open their books and read the questions in the list. Are any of their questions among them? Working individually, learners then read the text and answer the questions. Can they find answers for their own questions, as well?

➡ whisky/whiskey
The name of this drink comes from the Gaelic *uisge beatha*, which means 'water of life'. The Scottish variety is known as *Scotch* and spelt *whisky*. The Irish and US spelling is (usually) *whiskey*.

2a) Key
1. Michael Molloy
2. 12
3. Captain Bernard Daley
4. He expanded it and developed it.
5. 200
6. 2,000,000

2b)

Get learners to cover the text and complete the sentences, using words from the list. When they have finished, they can check with the text. Ask them to underline any words or phrases they are uncertain about, then call them out. Elicit the meaning from other learners, if possible.

Draw learners' attention to the Memo on p. 16, which contains very useful language for talking about numbers. Check that learners have understood the phrases properly by asking how many of them mean the same thing (two: *almost 100; just under 100.*). If they had to choose one of the phrases to cover all eventualities, which would it be? *(around 100).*

2b) Key
1. The Tullamore company **produces** whiskey.
2. The first **owner** of the company was Michael Molloy.
3. Michael Molloy **employed** twelve people.
4. Bernard Daley **took over** the company when Molloy died.
5. Daniel Williams **ran** the company for many years.
6. The present **workforce** is over 250 people.

3a)

Tell learners they are going to hear a guide at Tullamore Dew just starting his tour. Their task it to listen and find three details that differ from the information in the text on p. 15.

Ask learners to close their books and simply listen the first time around. Perhaps they will already be able to discern one or two differences. Next, ask them to open their books and look again at the text on p. 15. Play the recording again and learners compare what they hear with the written text. They can underline differences as they hear them. If necessary, play the recording once more. Then ask for feedback and gather the differences on the board. Play the recording once more and learners compare what is on the board with what they hear.

CD 1/6
See the tapescript on p. 187 of the Learner's Book.

Holiday problems

Unit summary

The topics of this unit are lost property procedures and reporting a theft to the police. The grammar revises and contrasts the Present perfect and Past simple tenses. The Past progressive is introduced in the second part of the unit.

Part A: I've lost my handbag

Focus
The London Transport Lost Property Office
Describing lost property
Different kinds of materials

Functions
Expressing regret: *Oh, dear.*
Asking for information: *What's it made of?*
Describing something: *It's made of ...; It's just a normal ...*

Grammar
Present perfect vs. Past simple (Revision)

What you need
Unit 2A, 5b): One photocopy of p. 113 for every three learners in the class.

1 Revision: Present perfect simple vs. progressive

In this activity learners use the Present perfect simple and the Present perfect progressive to describe what people have just done/have just been doing. As the people in the picture have not been numbered, learners will have to describe the person, then say what he/she has done/has been doing (see the Key).

Before starting, look at the picture with the class and get them to agree on what it shows. Working in pairs, learners then write their descriptions of the activities they can see. Before asking learners for their contributions write *Present perfect (simple)* and *Present perfect progressive* on the board. Gather their sentences under the appropriate heading.

1 Key
Some possibilities:
The young man on the right has been to a football match.
Someone has stolen
- his wallet.
- his mobile phone.

The couple on the left have been sightseeing.
The woman
- has bought a camera.
- has been taking photos.

The man in the blue jacket
- has been phoning.
- has stolen the young man's mobile phone.

Someone has been doing a lot of shopping.
The man with the moustache has bought a CD.

2a)

Before commencing with this activity, you could ask if anyone in the group has had personal experience with a Lost Property Office. What did they lose and where? Was it lost or stolen? Did they get it back?

Learners then work in pairs and make a list of five items they think the London Lost Property Office might receive a lot of.

2a) Key
Learners' own suggestions

2b)

Learners read the text and check the articles on their own list against it. Ask learners what other items they had on their list that were not mentioned in the text.

You might want to focus on two of the items in the text: *sets of keys* and *pairs of glasses*. Elicit the singular form of each, i.e. *a set of keys, a pair of glasses.* Can learners think of other examples similar to these? (*pairs of gloves, pairs of socks, pairs of trousers*).

➥ Sherlock Holmes

The great detective appears in four novels and fifty-six stories by the Scottish writer (and doctor) Sir Arthur Conan Doyle (1859 – 1930). According to his creator, Holmes shared lodgings upstairs at 221B in London's Baker Street with his friend and collaborator Doctor Watson, and was cared for by their faithful housekeeper Mrs Hudson. On retiring, Holmes moved down to Sussex, where he kept bees. The Sherlock Holmes Museum in Baker Street is said to receive about 50 letters a week, enquiring after Holmes or seeking his services.

2c)

Ask learners to look at the four statements/questions. Working individually, they then read the text again for detail.

2c) Key
1. the Sherlock Holmes house at 221B Baker Street and The Lost Property Office of London Transport
2. bus, train, taxi, underground

3. between 3,500 and 4,200 items each week (500 to 600 items each day)
4. a four-metre boat, a briefcase with 10,000 pounds, a wedding dress, a kitchen sink

3a)

Tell learners they will now hear a dialogue between a man working at the Lost Property Office and a woman who is looking for a lost item.

Ask learners to read the questions. Then play the dialogue and learners answer the three questions.

CD 1/9

See the tapescript on pp. 187 of the Learner's Book.

3a) Key

1. She lost it yesterday afternoon around three o'clock.
2. It's black.
3. There was a bit of money and some keys in it.

3b)

This is a listening activity with an unusual twist to it. First, ask learners to read the dialogue and make a mental note of words/phrases they think could be missing. As they have just heard the recording, they may well remember much of the text. They should, however, **not write** in the missing words.

Now, play the recording again and learners read along, **mentally noting** the missing language. Then, working with a partner, they practise the dialogues, adding the missing words as they speak. Allow them sufficient time for practice, then ask a pair to play the dialogue for the class.

3b) Key (for your information only!)

How can I **help you**?
I've lost my **handbag**.
Where did you **lose it**?
And can you describe your **handbag** for **me**?
Well, it's just a normal **handbag**.
Well, what colour **is it**?
Black, I **think**.
And is there anything **inside** it?
Just a bit of **money** and some keys.

3c)

Ask learners to cover the dialogue before commencing with this task. They now work individually and put the words in order to make the attendant's questions. (Note that these questions are not an exact reproduction of what learners heard in the recording.) When everyone has finished, carry on to the next task, which complements this one.

3c) Key

1. Can you describe it for me?
2. What's it made of?
3. What colour is it?
4. What make is it?
5. Is there anything inside it?

3d)

With the dialogue still covered, learners try to write Mrs Lopez's answers to the questions in 3c). Tell them not to worry if they can't remember the exact wording. If they can remember the basic information, that is fine.

Go directly on to the next step without checking.

3d) Key

1. It's just a normal handbag.
2. Plastic, I think. Or it could be leather. Yes, it's made of leather.
3. Black, I think. Or is it brown? No, it's black.
4. I've no idea. I bought it at Mark's and Spencer's, I think.
5. Just a bit of money and some keys.

3e)

Play the recording and learners check their answers against what they hear. Tell them they will hear the answers in a slightly different order. In the recording (and dialogue text) the order is 1,3,2,4,5.

Now draw learners' attention to the Grammar box. Here, the Present perfect (simple) is contrasted with the Past simple tense.

3e) Key

Grammar box:
Present perfect
Past simple

4a)

Ask learners to look at the list of items. Pronounce each word and get learners repeat them after you. Then, they work individually and match the words with the pictures.

4a) Key

1. handbag, 2. umbrella, 3. briefcase, 4. wallet, 5. rucksack, 6. gloves, 7. (cigarette) lighter, 8. headphones, 9. digicam

4b)

Read the sentences aloud. Learners then add the item being described. Even if they do not know all the words in the sentences, there should be enough information for them to get it right.

progressive, with which Mr Kahn reports those (now past) observations to the police. This is confirmed by the Grammar box that follows 2d).

2b) Key

1. happened, 2. was sitting, 3. stole, 4. was looking, 5. was taking, 6. were having, 7. was taking, 8. took

2c)

Play the recording. Learners check their work.

CD 1/13

See the dialogue in 2b) and the key to 2b).

2d)

In pairs, learners practise the dialogue.

Next ask them to look at the picture on p. 25 again. There they can see that Mr Kahn is reading the newspaper. But if they turn to the picture in 2b), they are in the police station where Mr Kahn is reporting something that is now in the past, so he says he **was** reading the newspaper.

Now draw learners' attention to the Grammar box. Ask them to read the first two sentences and complete the sentence below the box.

Finally, ask someone to read out the third sentence in the Grammar box. Focus on the two verbs: *was reading* and *stole*. Why do they think two different tenses are being used here? Which of the two actions was the shorter?

Learners might find a diagram helpful here. Draw a line on the board and write *Past* at the left-hand end and *Now* at the right-hand end. Above the line write *He was reading the newspaper*. Mark an X on the line below the sentence and write *stole* beneath the X. In other words, the Past simple is used for an action which occurs during a longer activity.

2d) Key

Zeit

Vergangenheit

3a)

Play the recording, stopping after each word so that learners can repeat it.

➡ pronouncing /w/

In standard British English there is now normally no difference between the pronunciation of the *w-* in *wear* and the *wh-* in *where*. Some speakers, particularly in Scotland, Ireland and the USA, still aspirate the *wh-*, so that words like *where, when, while* and *white* sound like *hwere, hwen, hwile* and *hwite*. (This feature does not apply to *who(m), whose, whole, whore.)*

CD 1/14

See the six words in 3a).

3b)

Learners now practise the sounds in sentences. Play the recording, stopping it after each sentence. Ask learners to repeat individually. Individual practice will be useful here, as this is a sound which German speakers often mispronounce.

CD 1/15

See the four sentences in 3b).

4a)

Ask learners to look at the four pictures, allowing them sufficient time to detect any differences in the illustrations. With the exception of one very slight difference in picture B (the man at the table sitting on the right is watching something rather than taking a photo, as depicted in A,C and D) all the differences concern Olivia's activities and the position of her handbag.

Tell learners they will now hear another dialogue at the police station, where Olivia is reporting the theft of her handbag to the officer on duty. Play the recording and learners tick the correct picture.

CD 1/16

See the tapescript on p. 188 of the Learner's Book.

4a) Key

Picture C

4b)

Ask learners to read the statement. Deal with any words that require clarification, then play the recording and learners mark their answers. As the recording is rather long, you might wish to break it up into smaller segments by making use of the pause button. Play the recording a second time if necessary.

Some learners might query the use of the Past progressive in the second sentence, where it is used to describe both actions. In this example, both actions took place simultaneously over a longer period of time.

Ask if learners can correct the false statements.

4b) Key

True: 4, 5, 7

False: 1, 2, 3, 6, 8

4c)

Learners now work with a partner. Each describes a picture and the other tries to guess which picture it is.

Before they start, ask them to look at the prompt box and point out that they should try to use the Past progressive and the Past simple as often as possible. This will be easier if their descriptions begin with the general and move on to the more specific.

4c) Key

Learners' own descriptions

4d)

In this activity learners personalise the language they have learnt.

Write four questions on the board: *What? Where? When? What happened?* Give learners some time to make a note of what they would like to say. Then ask them, in turn, to relate their experiences.

⚠

Don't correct learners' grammar while they are speaking! This activity involves genuine communication, so grammatical accuracy is not the top priority. You could make notes as learners relate their experiences, then make general comments/corrections at the end of the activity.

5a)

Ask learners to take a sheet of paper and write down the five times, leaving enough space between each one for several notations. They then walk around and interview each other, noting the name and activities of the people they talked with. They should interview several people, asking each of them all the questions, as they will need this information for the next activity.

5b)

Ask learners to look at the prompt box, then make statements based on the information gleaned from their interviews, e.g. *I talked to Maria, Marc and Anna. I think … is the busiest. For example…*

6a)

Lost in France was Bonnie Tyler's first successful recording. The lyrics are set to a whimsical melody which gives the song a meaning the words alone cannot express.

Learners work in pairs and decide which words words might fit best in the gaps.

➡ **Bonnie Tyler**

Bonnie Tyler (real name Gaynor Hopkins) was born into a large Welsh family in 1951 and starting singing with pop groups as a teenager. Soon after recording *Lost in France* she underwent an operation on her vocal chords. She started speaking again soon afterwards – against doctor's orders – with the result that her already powerful voice took on a rough edge which has made her one of the most distinctive female singers of the rock/pop scene. Perhaps her best-known song is *It's a heartache*.

6a) Key

Learners' own guesses

6b)

Play the recording and learners check their work.

Additionally, you could ask learners to look through the lyrics again and underline all the examples of the Past progressive they can find. (*birds were singing; day was just beginning; band was playing; they were saying; he was standing there; vines were over-flowing; stars were glowing*)

CD 1/17

See the tapescript on p. 188 of the Learner's Book.

6b) Key

1. birds, 2. day, 3. rain, 4. danced, 5. standing, 6. million, 7. telephone

Food

Unit summary

This unit focuses on favourite recipes, cooking and ingredients, as well as the styles of food offered in different kinds of restaurants. Grammar features the verbs *must/mustn't* and *don't have to* and also revises various forms of comparison. Learners also write a favourite recipe in English.

Part A: You mustn't forget to add the sauce

Focus
Food items
Recipes and cooking language
Favourite recipes
Writing instructions

Functions
Giving instructions: *Add a teaspoon ...; You must chop the mushrooms ...*
Reminding someone to do something: *You mustn't forget to add the sauce.*
Offering alternatives: *If you don't like the mushrooms, you don't have to use them. Use carrots if you prefer.*

Grammar
must / mustn't
don't have to

Pronunciation
Sounds:
/ʌ/ as in u̲p
/ɒ/ as in cho̲p

What you need:
Unit 3A, 6a): One photocopy of p. 114 for each learner.

1 Revision: Past simple and Past progressive

In this activity, learners revise the Past simple and Past progressive. On the board, write: *He was walking the dog when he met a friend.* What are the two tenses? Why are they different?

Now ask learners to look at the prompt box at the bottom of the page. Get one learner to read out the first example sentence and another to read out the reactions to it. Repeat with the second sentence.

In pairs, learners then take it in turns to create meaningful sentences using the phrases supplied. If they are in doubt about the grammatical correctness of any of their sentences, they should write them down.

When the activity has finished, call for any sentences learners were uncertain about.

2a)

Before learners begin the pair work, check the pronunciation of the items in the list. Read each word and let learners repeat after you. *Worcestershire sauce* ['wʊstəʃə 'sɔːs] will undoubtedly be the most difficult one in the list!

Learners then work in pairs and translate the food items into German.

➡ Worcestershire sauce
Often shortened to Worcester ['wʊstə] sauce, this is a strongly-flavoured, bottled brown sauce that is used with beef dishes, in particular, and is an essential ingredient in a Bloody Mary. It is made of vinegar, molasses, corn syrup, water, chilli peppers, soy(a) sauce, pepper, tamarinds, anchovies, onions, shallots, cloves and garlic.

2a) Key
bacon – (Frühstücks-) Speck
broccoli – Broccoli
butter – Butter
carrots – Möhren
cheese – Käse
garlic – Knoblauch
ham – Schinken
milk – Milch
minced beef – Hackfleisch
mushrooms – Champignons/Pilze
onions – Zwiebeln
peas – Erbsen
pepper – Pfeffer
potatoes – Kartoffeln
prawns – Garnelen
salt – Salz
tomatoes – Tomaten
Worcestershire sauce – no adequate translation!

2b)

Shepherd's Pie is a simple dish which is very popular in Britain. Not only is it tasty and easy to make, but it also has the advantage that one can easily substitute ingredients when preparing it.

The chef on the radio cookery show talks about his own recipe for Shepherd's Pie and how he prepares it. Learners listen to the recording and tick the items from the list that the chef mentions. If necessary, play the recording a second time.

CD 1/18
See the tapescript on pp. 188-9 of the Learner's Book.

2b) Key

butter, cheese, milk, minced beef, mushrooms, onions, pepper, potatoes, salt, Worcestershire sauce

3a)

Ask learners to look at the pictures, which illustrate the different steps in preparing the dish. Then ask them to look at the list of instructions. Read each one and ask learners to read after you. Don't translate them at this point, however. The images contain enough information to allow proper matching with the text.

Learners now work individually and match the sentences and the pictures.

3a) Key

b add a teaspoon of Worcestershire sauce
g sprinkle the grated cheese over the pie
a peel the potatoes with a knife
c slice the mushrooms
i boil the potatoes in water
h drain the potatoes
f mash the potatoes with a fork
e chop the onions into small pieces
d fry the minded beef until it is brown

3b)

This recording is a continuation of the radio show. Play the recording. Learners look at the pictures in 3a) and number the steps in the order they are mentioned. Check by asking learners to read them in the proper order.

Now ask learners to look at the bubbles in the picture at the bottom of the page. Draw attention to the two verbs, *mustn't/don't have to*, and elicit their meanings. What is the German equivalent for *mustn't*? (*darf/dürfen nicht*) And for *don't have to*? (*muss/müssen nicht*)

Leave it at this for the moment. The two structures will be focused on later in the unit.

CD 1/19

See the tapescript on p. 189 of the Learner's Book.

3b) Key

a1, b8, c7, d6, e5, f4, g9, h3, i2

1 peel the potatoes with a knife
2 boil the potatoes in water
3 drain the potatoes
4 mash the potatoes with a fork
5 chop the onions into small pieces
6 slice the mushrooms
7 fry the minced beef until it is brown
8 add a teaspoon of Worcestershire sauce
9 sprinkle the grated cheese over the pie

3c)

This is the chef's recipe for the cheese and mushroom Shepherd's Pie. Ask learners to work in pairs, read the recipe, then guess the meaning of the words in italics and translate them below . Tell them not to worry about the blanks — these will be filled in in the next step.

3c) Key

1. reicht für sechs Personen
2. Viertel
3. Eßlöffel
4. goldbraun
5. feuerfeste Form
6. oben drauf
7. vorgeheizt
8. verschmolzen
9. servieren

3d)

Play the recording again. Learners now complete the recipe by filling in the numbers they hear.

⚠

The recording is not identical to the text on the page.

Direct learners' attention to the Grammar box. Ask them to read the examples. Elicit the meanings of each of the verbs in italics. Then ask them to consider the forms of each of the two verbs. Are they alike in all six persons? (*mustn't:* yes; *don't have to:* no (*he/she doesn't have to*). The third person singular form will not be actively used here, so you needn't dwell further on the point.

Finally, ask learners to fill in the blanks in the text.

3d) Key

Recipe:

- 5; 25; 50
- 2
- 750; 200
- –
- –
- 450; 15
- 200
- –

Grammar box:

mustn't = nicht **dürfen**
don't have to = nicht **müssen**.

4

In this pronunciation exercise, learners focus on the difference between two vowel sounds:
/ʌ/ as in *up* and /ɒ/ as in *chop*.

Write the symbols on the board, along with an example of each one. Repeat the two words and get learners to repeat after you.

Play the recording, stopping after each sentence for learners to repeat, either in chorus or individually, as you think best.

CD 1/20
See the sentences in step 4.

5a)

Learners read the mother's kitchen rules, then complete them with one of the three verbs supplied. Check by asking individual learners to read the rules.

5a) Key
1. must, 2. mustn't, 3. must, 4. don't have to, 5. mustn't, 6. must, 7. mustn't, 8. mustn't, 9. don't have to, 10. must

5b)

Learners now work in pairs and discuss how they feel about these rules. Are they good ones or are they too strict? Perhaps learners have completely different rules they would like to mention. They should use the phrases in the prompt box at the top of the right-hand column.

When they have finished, ask the pairs to share their views.

5c)

Learners now personalise the language and write a list of rules (no more than four or five) for a room in their own house for an English-speaking guest (e.g. a young exchange student, as *must/mustn't* would be inappropriate forms to use with an adult guest). If they haven't got any fixed rules in operation, they could simply make some up.

When they have finished their lists, ask them to get together in groups of three and take it in turns to read their lists to each other.

6a)

Everyone has their own speciality – something they particularly like to prepare, or, if they don't cook themselves, something someone else makes and they particularly enjoy eating.

Using the model in 3c) learners write their own recipe and cooking instructions. You might prefer to give them a photocopy of p. 114 to write their recipe on, rather than doing it in the book.

The recipe should include:
1. the name of the dish;
2. how many people it serves;
3. a list of ingredients, including the amount of each ingredient;
4. instructions for preparation, including anything special, e.g. a secret for success.

⚠
Learners will probably not have enough information on hand to complete this activity successfully ad hoc, so you might prefer to give it as a homework assignment. This would have the advantage that those who don't cook themselves could find a recipe they would like to present.

6b)

Learners talk about their recipes in this activity.
First, ask them to work in groups of four or five and exchange recipes. They can talk about them and pass them around to each other for perusal. They should note down any recipes they think they'd like to try themselves. After a few minutes, ask them to talk to other people and look at their recipes. Let this continue until each learner has talked to at least two or three other people.

6c)

If learners are interested, you could collect the recipes and make a 'class recipe book'. If you have access to a photocopier, make copies of the book for everyone.

Part B: I'd rather eat Italian

Focus
Waiter-customer dialogues
Restaurant advertisements
Different types of food
Comparing restaurants

Functions
Estimating: *... can expect to pay around ... per person.*
Advising: *Booking is a good idea.*
Accepting a suggestion: *That sounds fine to me; Great.*
Rejecting a suggestion: *No, not Indian again, Steve, please!*
Seeking consensus: *OK – let's not argue!; Is everyone happy with that?*
Suggesting: Listen, why don't we ...;
Expressing frustration: *Please – let's just choose one!*

Grammar
Comparison (Revision): *milder than; more expensive than; better than; the same as; different from; not as spicy as*

1a) Revision: restaurant phrases

This part of the unit focuses on restaurants and eating out. Working individually, learners read the phrases and decide who would normally say them: customer or waiter/waitress. Get the class to agree, then focus on pronunciation.

Ask learners to work in pairs and practise saying the phrases as naturally as possible, as they would do in the actual situation. (To avoid them all working on the same phrase and distracting each other, start one pair on no. 1, one on no. 3, one on no. 5, etc.)

You might ask learners to comment on the last phrase. Has anyone ever gone to a restaurant and been turned away because their dress was too casual? It is not uncommon for better restaurants in English-speaking countries to require their male customers to wear a jacket and tie.

1a) Key
1. customer, 2. customer, 3. waiter, 4. waiter, 5. customer, 6. customer, 7. waiter, 8. waiter

1b)

Learners now work in pairs and create mini-dialogues, using the phrases in 1a) as openers. After they have had sufficient time to practise, ask each pair to perform a different dialogue. There may well be several alternatives for some of them.

1b) Key
Some possibilities:
1. Our food hasn't come yet.
   I'm sorry. I'll ask in the kitchen.
2. A table for two, please – smoking.
   Right. This way, please.
3. Is everything OK?
   Yes, thank you.
4. Try the chef's pâté. It's delicious.
   That's a good idea.
5. Can I pay by credit card?
   Yes, of course.
6. We've been waiting for a table for over an hour.
   It will only be a moment now. You're next.
7. You don't have to make a reservation. We're not busy tonight.
   Great!
8. I'm sorry sir – all our customers have to wear a jacket.
   Oh! I didn't know that.

2a)

In this activity learners skim the reading texts for detail. It is important that they do the tasks **one at a time**. This means they will skim the texts, or at least part of the texts, six times before they have finished the exercise.

When they have found their answer to a task, they move on to the next, but should begin their skimming with the first text again, working their way through them all until they have found the answer for the relevant statement.

By working in this manner, learners become quite familiar with the information, far more so than if they were to take a less disciplined approach. Remind them that it is not important to understand every word in the texts. Here, they are just looking for certain details.

Before they start, tell them they have five minutes to find all the information. This will force them to read quickly without worrying too much about unfamiliar language.

2a) Key
1. Brown's
2. Amanda's
3. Al's Place
4. The Lotus Flower
5. Brown's
6. Al's Place

2b)

This task requires a closer reading of the individual restaurant descriptions. Learners read through the texts and mark the statements true or false. Ask them to also underline the segment of the text which confirms their choice.

2b) Key
True: 1, 2, 3
False: 4, 5

2c)

Ask learners to look at the list of adjectives describing food. Elicit the meanings of the words from the learners. *Spicy* food can also be called *hot*, which is the word that many native speakers would use. There is a slight difference between *heavy* and *filling*. *Heavy* is often used to describe dishes with lots of butter or cream, such as cream cake, or meals with meat, sauce and potatoes. A dish can be healthy and *filling*, however, without being *heavy*.

Learners work individually and write in the name of a dish or type of food (not necessarily from the restaurant ads) that they think suits each adjective. The foods in the green box below may help 'non-foody' learners to get started!

2c) Key
Learners' own opinions

2d)

Food interest almost everyone, so in order to get maximum mileage from the vocabulary on these pages, you might like to set this up as a group activity. Scatter the seven adjectives across the board, then choose one and ask learners to call out their examples. To keep it lively, write only those items that seem to be new to most people. To keep learners alert during the activity, tell them they should write down two things they were not previously familiar with.

3a)

Ask learners to close their books. Tell them they are going to hear a conversation between an English teacher, Steve, and his three foreign friends Nina, Inga and Ralf. The four want to go out for a meal and are trying to agree on a restaurant. Learners listen to the recording to find out where they finally decide to eat.

CD 1/21
See the tapescript on p. 189 of the Learner's Book.

3a) Key
Al's Place

3b)

Ask learners to open their books, look at the picture and read the speech bubbles. How many ways of comparing things can they find? (There are two: *the same as*, and *different from.)*. What does *I'd rather go to a Thai restaurant* express? (It implies a preference, e.g. *I'd rather go to a Thai restaurant than to an Indian one.*
Draw learners' attention to the Memo.

Learners now work individually and complete the text. In this case no words are supplied for learners to choose from, but the context is clear and the missing language can be filled in easily.

3b) Key
1. rather, 2. same, 3. from, 4. as, 5. don't, 6. expensive, 7. more, 8. than, 9. better, 10. hungry

3c)

Play the recording and learners check their answers.

This conversation offers a good example of the consensus-finding process. In many respects, it is much like a ritual; a conversation like this normally passes through several phases before the participants reach a conclusion. Such a process is also very culture bound, and it is important that learners are aware of the 'English' process, which might be different from what they are used to in their own culture.

Ask learners to read through the dialogue with a partner and try to identify the phases of the conversation and the essential language used in each phase.

Gather feedback and channel it into the following categories, adding the phrases as they are mentioned:

Opening
The topic is introduced:
So … where shall we go and eat today?

Suggesting and reacting to suggestions
The general discussion takes place and opinions are exchanged:
There are some nice restaurants; These look quite good; It's highly recommended. Let's go there; No, not Indian again!; I'd rather go to …; That sounds fine to me; They say it's very good.

Decision making
Which phrases end the general discussion and lead to the final decision?
OK – let's not argue! Listen, why don't we go to this place?
(The choice has now been limited, but there is still room for discussion.)
Please – let's just choose one! I'm hungry.
(Frustration is setting in and a decision must be made.)

Approving a decision
Which phrases express approval?
Is everyone happy with that?; That's fine; Great; So, let's go.

Ask learners if they think the process of consensus finding is very different in their own culture. If so, what are the differences?

Now play the recording again and learners turn their attention to stress and intonation. They should listen for the characteristics that make the dialogue sound lively. Working in groups of four, they practise the dialogue, trying to keep it as authentic as possible. One way to achieve this (and have a bit of fun at the same time) is to exaggerate each role somewhat, i.e. really play the part.

4a)

Focus on the Grammar box, which revises comparisons. Ask learners to read the comparisons and decide what they all have in common. (Two things are being compared with each other in various ways.)

➡ **Comparison of *different***

British English: *different from/different to*

American English: *different than.*

Now ask learners to look at the prompt box. Learners practise simple exchanges, asking for preferences and giving reasons for their choices.

4a) Key

Learners' own questions and responses

4b)

Learners now personalise the language they have learnt. Working in groups of three or four, they either decide on one of the restaurants on p. 35 or choose a restaurant in their own town.

Ask them to look at the prompt box, which collects some of the consensus-finding structures they have been working with. Remind them of the various phases of the consensus-finding process and tell them they should try to structure their discussion with this in mind.

4c)

Ask the groups to report their results. Which restaurant did they choose and why? Was it easy to reach a decision that everyone was happy with?

Now draw learners' attention to the *TIPP für erfolgreiche Kommunikation*. This information sums up some of the language used in consensus finding and focuses on the phrases that might be most useful. It also lists some of the phases that a consensus-finding process takes: opening, suggestion making and discussion, making the final decision, general acceptance of the decision.

Self-check

Following every third unit in Fairway is a 'Self-check' section. These sections allow learners to monitor their progress at regular intervals throughout the course. Look at this first one together with your class.

Each Self-check tests the material presented in the preceding three units. Learners can check their results in the Keys section at the back of their Student's Books (pp. 173 – 186).

Draw attention to the checklist at the end of the section („Mein Lernfortschritt"). This is designed to motivate learners by identifying the tasks they can now carry out in English.

All the five Self-checks are based on TELC mock exams. We hope that learners will be motivated to take the B1 Certificate in English exam on completion of Fairway 3.

The world of film and music

Unit summary

This unit focuses on film and music. In the first part of the unit learners read a film review and talk about different kinds of films. The second part of the unit focuses on concerts and ordering tickets by telephone, and includes an e-mail about a concert. The main grammar features are the Present simple passive and reflexive pronouns. Adjectives and adverbs are contrasted again (revision).

Part A: Will Lightman is played by Hugh Grant

Focus
Film reviews
Describing films: actors, directors, settings and music
Choosing a film to watch

Functions
Suggesting: *What about this?; I know. Let's ...*
Rejecting a suggestion: *No, I don't feel like ...-ing.*
Expressing frustration: *Oh, I give up.*
Expressing opinions: *I feel ...*
Asking for opinions: *What do you think of ...?*

Grammar
Present simple passive: *Will Lightman is played by Hugh Grant.*

Pronunciation
Sounds:
/æ/ as in p<u>a</u>t
/e/ as in p<u>e</u>t

1 Revision: making, accepting and rejecting suggestions

In this pair activity learners practise making suggestions, accepting them or making alternative suggestions. First ask them to read through the pairs of phrases and look at the prompt box below. In pairs, they then work through the list and either agree or make an alternative suggestion.

2a)

The reading text is a film review of 'About a Boy', a film released in January 2003. It is based on a novel of the same name by Nick Hornby. Before beginning the task, you might like to ask if anyone has seen the film or read the book, and if so, say a few words about it. Then brainstorm the types of information one would expect to find in a film review.

The review is fairly challenging but in this first activity learners only have to answer very general questions concerning Nick Hornby and the film.

Ask learners to read the questions. Remind them that their first reading of the text should be goal-oriented and that they should not worry too much about new words or structures that may seem difficult. They will become more familiar with the text in the steps that follow.

2a) Key
1. Yes
2. 'Four Weddings and a Funeral' and 'Notting Hill'
3. 'High Fidelity' and 'Fever Pitch'

2b)

Before learners read the TIPP at the top of the page, ask them how they deal with unfamiliar words in texts (apart from consulting a dictionary, which can be very time-consuming, and is often not necessary).

Now ask learners to read the TIPP, then look at the list of words in 2b). These are the words which are underlined in the text in the previous step. Learners should look back and the text and try to deduce the meanings of these words from the context, then mark the best meaning.

The Grammar box is dealt with in the next step.

2b) Key
1. a) at the cinema
2. b) money paid to a writer
3. c) to be in a serious relationship
4. b) character in the film
5. a) writing
6. b) emotional
7. b) try and see
8. a) similar to

3a)

This step presents and practises the Present simple passive.

Before commencing with the activity, ask learners to look at the Grammar box and read the sentences. What is the difference between them? There is no difference in meaning, but there is a difference in focus. In the first two examples (Active) the focus is on the subjects, *Hugh Grant* and *New actors*. In the second pair of examples (Passive) the focus is on *Will Lightman* and *Marcus and his mother*.

You might point out that passive forms are often found in certain types of written texts, such as reviews, reports and the like, where it is more important to present results than to mention agents (the thing or person doing an action). The Passive tense is less often used in spoken English.

Finally, ask learners to complete the sentence in German below the Grammar box.

Now, ask learners to look at the 'switchboard' at the top of the right-hand column. Do an example yourself, then ask learners to work in groups of three and make as many sentences as they can using only the language presented in the box.

➡ by

Note the frequent use of *by* in these sentences. This preposition is often used in passive clauses to introduce the agent, the person or thing that causes something to happen.

3a) Key

Grammar box:
be
dritten

Sentences (some possibilities):
Mr Bean is played by Rowan Atkinson.
The 'Star Wars' films are directed by George Lukas.
The song 'Yesterday' is sung by Paul McCartney.
The film 'The Man in the Iron Mask'
- is set in France / in the 17th century.
- is based on a story by Alexandre Dumas.
'New York, New York' is sung by Frank Sinatra.
Indiana Jones is played by Harrison Ford.
The film 'Bridget Jones' Diary' is based on a book by Helen Fielding.

3b)

In this activity learners note information about their favourite films. They do not need to answer all the questions. They simply make notes on the points they know about. If you sense that there are not too many film enthusiasts in the class, learners could work in pairs or groups of three and pool their knowledge.

3b) Key

Learners' own answers

3c)

If your learners worked in groups in 3b), you could do this activity as a class game. If they did 3b) individually, they can work in small groups here.

Ask learners to look at the bubble. Is this the active or passive form? What about the sentences in the prompt box below? Using these examples, learners create sentences about their film, then describe it to others in the group who try to guess the name of the film described.

4

Give the class a moment or two to read the instructions, then elicit the meanings of the various film genres by asking learners to describe the characteristics of each one, e.g. a *romantic comedy* is a love story that is also funny.

Learners then work in pairs and think of examples of each film type. When everyone has finished, call for a few examples of each one.

Some possibilities:
Thriller: *The Silence of the Lambs; Patriot Games*
Horror film: *Psycho, Scream*
Western: *High Noon; The Good, the Bad and the Ugly*
Epic: *Ben Hur; Gladiator*
Action film: *Terminator; Mission Impossible*
Comedy: *A Fish called Wanda; Johnny English*
Romantic comedy: *Notting Hill; Bridget Jones' Diary*
Drama: *Kramer versus Kramer; Capote*
Science fiction: *2001; War of the Worlds*

5a)

Present the two sounds with some clear simple examples, e.g.
/æ/ as, that, add
/e/ yes, best, get

Write the symbols and examples on the board, then get the class to chorus them several times after you.

Now ask learners to look at the words on the page. Play the recording, stopping after each example for learners to practise.

For more practice, write some further examples from the unit on the board and drill them:
/æ/ man, action, happy, character, camerawork, Atkinson
/e/ success, well, better, melody, yesterday, western

⚠

The second *a* in *character* and *camera* is usually pronounced /ə/ (schwa).

CD 1/23

See the six words in 5a).

5a) Key

/æ/ romantic, actor, badly
/e/ epic, director, set in

5b)

Learners now listen to the sentences and repeat. Play the recording, stopping after each sentence. Go round the class, asking each learner to repeat the sentence. Make corrections where necessary. You needn't ask learners to identify individual sounds in the words. The goal is to raise awareness of the difference in the two sounds.

CD 1/24
See the four sentences in 5b).

5b) Key
1. /æ/ sat, romantic
   /e/ excellent
2. /æ/ badly
   /e/ epic, directed
3. /æ/ action, Africa
   /e/ set, adventure
4. /æ/ hat
   /e/ Check, better, Eric's

6a)
Ask learners to close their books. Tell them they will hear Wendy and Thomas discussing how they would like to spend the evening. Play the recording. The task here is simply to find out what the couple decide to do in the end.

CD 1/25
See the dialogue in 6b) and the key to 6b).

6a) Key
In the end they decide to go home and watch TV.

6b)
Ask learners to open their books and look at the list of adjectives below the instruction. Pronounce them and get the class to repeat them. Leave the meanings open for the moment. Learners have already heard the dialogue, so they should be able to complete it even if they aren't familiar with all the words. Now, working individually, learners complete the dialogue using the adjectives from the list.

6b) Key
1. funny, 2. silly, 3. long, 4. boring, 5. predictable, 6. violent, 7. bloody, 8. scary, 9. soppy, 10. always the same

6c)
Play the recording again so that learners can check their answers. Before they begin practising the dialogue, make certain that the meanings of the words are now clear to everyone.

➡ funny
This is often used incorrectly by German speakers. Point out that it has two meanings, *comical*, as in the dialogue, and *strange/odd*. It is not the adjective of *fun*!

7a)
Learners to look back at the films they chose in 3b) and 4, then select adjectives they think would a) describe them well and b) not describe them well. Working in pairs they then exchange opinions on the films.

⚠ *feel*
Here the verb *feel* is used in the sense of *think*, whereas in the dialogue it occurred in the phrase *I don't feel like … ing*, in other words *I'm not in the mood for …*.

7b)
Ask learners first to look at the prompt box, then walk around and talk to a number of people about their views. Ask them to make a mental note of those who like the same kinds of film as they do. Ask a few learners to report on their findings.

Part B: I went by myself

Focus
Ordering concert tickets by telephone
Talking about musical and other events
Reading and writing an e-mail

Functions
Asking someone to speak up (on the phone): *I'm sorry, I can't hear you very well. Can you speak up, please?*
Asking for information: *Are there any tickets left for ...?; If I can just have your name, please.*
Playing for time: *I need to think about it carefully.*
Convincing someone of something: *OK, but (we're selling the tickets very fast).*
Consenting: *OK then, I'll (take two circles, please).*

Grammar
Adjectives of quality vs. adverbs of manner: *They're good seats; I can't hear you very well.*
Reflexive pronouns: *I enjoyed myself.*

1 Revision: telephoning skills

Before the lesson, compare the two white boxes, on pages 47 and 123. The information is not the same!

In this information-gap activity learners use telephoning skills they have already acquired to enquire about one of The Proms concerts at the Royal Albert Hall in London.

Before you begin the activity, ask what they know about The Proms (Promenade Concerts). Some of them may at least have seen or heard about The Last Night of the Proms, the flamboyant and patriotic concert that ends each Proms season. Some may even have even attended a Proms concert and could talk about their experiences. Tell the class they can learn more about The Proms in the Reading for Fun section on p. 51 of their books.

Start the activity by dividing the class into two groups, A and B. Get all the 'A' learners to move to one side of the room and all the 'B' learners to the other. Group A looks at the information on p. 47 and works out appropriate questions using the starter phrases in the prompt box. Group B does the same with the information and phrases on p. 123.

Each of the 'A' learners now chooses a partner in the 'B' group and does the telephoning activity with them. To make it seem more authentic, you could ask the learners to sit back to back.

You could also ask two learners who have mobiles to come forward, then phone each other and play the roles. This would add a little fun to the activity and would be the most authentic way of reviewing the language again.

2a)

Before you begin the activity, you might like to say a word about the seating arrangement at Royal Albert Hall. Perhaps those who have seen it on television could comment here, as well.

Tell learners they are going to hear a woman calling the Royal Albert Hall Box Office to enquire about tickets. Then ask them to cover the dialogue on the right-hand side of the page and read the four questions.

Play the recording and learners answer the questions. If necessary, play it a second time.

➡ Royal Albert Hall
The Royal Albert Hall was named in memory of Queen Victoria's husband, the German-born Prince Albert of Saxe-Coburg and Gotha, and is one of London's leading venues for music events. The hall itself is oval with a capacity of 5000. There is a round arena at ground level, which is standing space only during the last Proms concert. Around this, but somewhat elevated, are the stalls (rows of seats). Above them are two tiers of boxes, then the seats in the circle and finally the gallery, which is standing room only. When the hall is full, it is indeed a place with a very special atmosphere.

➡ Paying by credit card
It is quite customary to pay by credit card in Britain when booking theatre and concert tickets by telephone. This does not necessarily mean, however, that the amount will be booked immediately. Quite often one is asked for the name and number of the credit card, but the amount is actually booked through when the ticket is picked up on the evening of the concert, as is the case here.

2a) CD 1/26
See the dialogue in 2b) and the key to 2b).

2a) Key
1. two
2. £25 pounds each
3. by credit card
4. when she picks up the tickets

2b)

Ask learners to look at the list of words. Working individually they use them to complete the dialogue.

2b) Key
1. I'm sorry
2. well
3. properly
4. Yes, but
5. carefully
6. fast
7. OK, then
8. So
9. And how
10. If I can just

2c)

Play the recording and learners check their answers.

2d)

Learners now work in pairs and practise the dialogue.

Before going on to the next step, ask learners to look at the Grammar box on p. 48, which contrasts adjectives and adverbs. First, ask them to look at the examples in the upper half of the box.

Elicit the difference in usage. Adjectives describe nouns/pronouns, whereas adverbs are used to describe verbs (adjectives and other adverbs).

What about their position in the sentence? Adjectives often precede the word being modified, whereas adverbs generally follow the verb being modified.

Now focus on the lower half of the Grammar box. Elicit the rules exemplified here, i.e.
1. Most adverbs add *–ly* to the adjective form, e.g. *careful+ly.*
2. The adverb *well* is quite different in form from its adjective counterpart *good.*
3. Some adverbs do not add *-ly*, e.g. *fast, early, wrong, late, hard.*

Ask learners to read through the dialogue on p. 47 again and underline all the adverbs they can find (*well, properly, fast, better, carefully*).

3a)

The next series of activities centres around an e-mail in which a woman tells a friend about her experiences at a Proms concert.

Ask learners to look at the picture. How could the phrase in the bubble be expressed in German? *(Ich könnte mich ohrfeigen!; Ich könnte mir in den Hinten treten!)*

Learners then read the e-mail and answer the questions.

3a) Key
1. last night
2. She liked both the music and the concert hall.
3. After the concert she went and had a pizza.

3b)

Learners now read the e-mail for more information, then mark the sentences true or false. Ask them to underline the segment of the text which confirms their choice. Tell them not to worry about the abbreviations yet. They will be dealt with in the next activity.

3b) Key
True: 2, 4, 6
False: 1, 3, 5, 7, 8

3c)

Learners now match the phrases here with the corresponding abbreviations in the e-mail.

You might mention that abbreviations such as these are now frequently used in informal e-mails. It is, however, general consensus that one should use only the most common abbreviations, such as *asap* (*as soon as possible*), *FYI* (*for your information*), *BTW* (*by the way*), *BR* (*best regards*), and *pls* (*please*).

Finish by asking learners to look through the e-mail again and underline any words or phrases they still find difficult. Learners call them out and either you or other learners give the meaning.

3c) Key
1. BTW, 2. BFN, 3. RUOK, 4. IMO

3d)

Before starting work on this step, ask learners to look at the Grammar box in 3e). Focus on the three example sentences in the lower half of the box. What is the subject of the first sentence? *(I)*. What is the object? *(myself)*. Who are these people? (the same person). What about the other two sentences? (the same applies).

So the rule is? (Write it up on the board, or dictate it, with blanks):
'A reflexive pronoun is used when the (subject) and (object) of the sentence refer to the same people or things).'

Now ask learners to complete the sentence below the Grammar box (Ich habe es ***selbst*** gemacht), then read through the e-mail again. How many reflexive pronouns can they find? (There are eight.) Note that two of the pronouns are prefixed with by *(by myself, by himself).* This is explained in the Memo box at the bottom of p. 49.

➡ **Reflexive pronouns (for your information only!)**
Note that these pronouns are also used to emphasise

something: *Do it yourself.* There is no need to mention this use to learners yet.

Now start the activity. Learners work in pairs, one taking the role of Joanna, the other another of her friends who has not heard about the concert experience. 'The friend' asks as many questions about the evening as he/she can think of. Some possible starters are given in the prompt box. 'Joanna' answers all the questions using the information in the e-mail.

Remind learners to switch roles so that both partners have an opportunity to practise questions. If possible, the second person should not ask the same questions. The text contains so much detail that this should not prove too difficult.

3e)

Learners now personalise the language and talk about live music events they have been to.

Ask learners to look at the prompts above the Grammar box. Make certain they pronounce *live* /laɪv/ correctly. This adjective is often confused with the noun *life*, which is incorrect in this context.

Learners take it in turns to interview a partner about their music experience. They should ask as many different questions about the event (and what they did before and after it) as possible and note down a few interesting bits of information as well.

Wind up by asking learners to say what their partner talked about and mention two interesting details about the event.

3e) Key

Grammar box:
selbst

4a)

Ask learners to look at the list of events, all of which should be familiar to them. Each of the sentences describes something about the event and some of the sentences could apply to more than one event.

Working individually, learners write in the types of events which suit the statements. Finally, ask learners to look through the statements once more and underline all the adverbs they can find. What verbs do they modify?

4a) Key

1. All the options are possible.
2. ballet
3. lecture
4. play, opera
5. football match
6. political meeting
7. football match
8. poetry reading, lecture
9. opera
10. All the options are possible.

4b)

Learners write an e-mail describing an event they have attended, either to you or to an English-speaking friend. They can choose anything from the list in 4a). Their e-mail should cover all the points listed in the questions.

This is a task learners will want to prepare carefully, so it might be well to give it as a homework assignment rather than devoting a great deal of class time to writing.

If possible, ask learners to send the e-mail to you when they have finished it. If they prefer to write to someone else, they could bring you a copy of the mail to the next lesson.

Correct the e-mails you receive. Discuss mistakes in the form of a general feedback at the beginning of the next session. If you find that learners are having problems with particular structures, such as adverbs, you might want to review the structure once more, using examples from the e-mails you received.

3b)

Play the recording and learners check their work. Then, play the recording again, pausing after each word for learners to practise.

4

Working in groups, learners discuss appropriate answers to the eight questions about politics in their own country and report their views on questions 7 and 8.

If you have an international group, learners could talk about the situation in the countries they are from as well. This additional information could be included in the general feedback.

4 Key

Learners' own answers

5a)

Ask learners to look at the two pictures. What types of events are the reporters going to be talking about? (the upper picture shows the Manchester United Football Club stadium before a match; the lower shows St Basil's Cathedral on Red Square in Moscow, where the G8 summit meeting is being held.)

What do learners know about the G8? Ask them to look at the picture on p. 52. What's happening in the picture? What do they think the posters mean? (The picture shows a demonstration in the Scottish capital Edinburgh during the 2005 G8 meeting which was held at the Gleneagles Hotel in Perthshire. The posters mean 'Turn poverty into a thing of the past'.)

➡ G8

G8 stands for meetings of the 'Group of Eight' nations. The first meeting of this kind took place in 1975 when the French President, Giscard d'Estaing, invited the leaders of Japan, the USA, Germany, the UK and Italy to Rambouillet, near Paris, to discuss the economic problems of the day. This G6 group was later expanded to include Canada, then Russia. The G8 has neither a fixed structure nor a permanent administration. The country that has the Presidency sets up the agenda and organises the annual G8 Summit, where a wide range of political, social and economic issues are discussed.

Learners now turn back to p. 54. Ask them to look at the prompt box below the pictures and imagine they are the reporters who are speaking. What more can they say about the locations/events in the pictures? They should use the Present progressive tense for this. Gather their contributions on the board.

5a) Key

Learners' own ideas

5b)

Learners now look at the phrases and decide whether they are more likely to hear them in connection with 1) the sporting event or 2) the political meeting, and number them accordingly.

5b) Key

Learners' own ideas

5c)

Play the recording and learners check their work.

CD 1/29

See the tapescripts on pp. 189-190 of the Learner's Book.

5c) Key

Report 1:
are arriving, are playing, are wearing, are hoping

Report 2:
are meeting, are discussing, are making progress, are having lunch

5d)

Ask learners to read the questions, then play the recordings again. Learners write the answers as they hear them. Stop between the reports to allow learners to finish writing. If necessary, play the recording a second time.

Now ask learners to look at the Grammar box, which contrasts the Present simple with the Present progressive. Learners should be quite familiar with these two tenses by now, but check that they have completed the sentences below correctly.

5d) Key

Report 1:
1. England and North Ireland are playing.
2. They're playing in Manchester.
3. The match starts at seven forty-five.

Report 2:
1. They're discussing poor African countries.
2. Right now they're having lunch at the presidential palace.
3. After today, they have three more days of meetings.

Grammar box:
Present simple
Present progressive

6a)

Learners now contrast the Present simple and the Present progressive by creating sentences about their classroom surroundings, e.g. describing how things usually are, compared with the way they are as they speak.

Ask learners to write down two sentences of their own, then read them out. Get the class to confirm that the tenses are being used accurately in each of the examples.

6b)

Ask learners to look at the prompt box and make similar sentences about what their friends or family might be doing at the time of speaking. They then take it in turns to tell a partner what they have written, and why.

7

Learners now work in groups of three or four and write a short newspaper article about a person everyone is familiar with.

Tell them they can make their article as wild and imaginative as they care to. Their article should, however, include a number of uses of the Present progressive. At the outset of the activity, each group should designate a group secretary. The secretary makes notes and writes the article in the final form for presentation.

When the groups have had sufficient time to complete their articles, ask either the group secretary or another member of the group to read the article to the class. During the presentation phase you should make notes, paying particular attention to the proper use of the verb tenses. After all the articles have been read, give the group general feedback.

Part B: The hotel we're staying in is OK

Focus
Olympic sports
Olympic Games in Athens
Keeping a weblog
Reporting

Functions
Expressing dislike: *I don't really like …*

Grammar
Defining relative clauses: *We went to the place that/ which makes the best kebabs in Athens.*
Clauses where the pronoun can be dropped: *The hotel (that/which) we're staying in is OK.*

1a) Revision: Present progressive

Tell learners they will hear a telephone conversation between two men. Ask them to read the questions, then answer them while you play the recording. If necessary, play the recording a second time.

CD 1/30
See the tapescript on p. 190 of the Learner's Book.

1a) Key
1. He's standing in the check-in queue at Heathrow Airport.
2. He's flying to Athens.
3. He's going to the Olympic Games.

1b) Revision: Present progressive

Learners use the information gleaned from the recording in 1a) and complete the sentences with the missing verbs.

When everyone has finished, play the recording again and learners check their answers.

1b) Key
I'm **standing** in the check-in queue.
I'm **flying** to **Athens**.
I'm **going** to **the Olympic Games** with Beth.
The woman's **calling** us to the check-in now.
I'm **making** breakfast.
We're going to **write** an Olympic blog every day on my website.

2a)

The next series of steps deals with various aspects of the Olympic Games and Olympic sports. First, ask learners to look at the list of sports. Pronounce each one and ask them to repeat after you. Learners then match the names of the various sports to the pictures.

➡ Olympic disciplines
Golf is not an Olympic discipline, but it is a sport which is recognised by the International Olympic Committee. The International Sports Federations that administer such sports must ensure that their statutes, practice and activities conform with the Olympic charter.

If you or your learners would like to find out more about the Olympics and Olympic disciplines, visit the official website: www.olympic.org

➡ athletics
This is also known as track and field.

2a) Key
1. badminton, 2. golf, 3. gymnastics, 4. marathon, 5. volleyball, 6. hockey, 7. athletics (also known as track and field), 8. show jumping, 9. wrestling, 10. swimming, 11. archery, 12. rowing

2b)

Beth and Dan have arrived in Athens and are talking to the hotel owner about the availability of tickets for various events. They have already got some tickets, but would like more. Play the recording and learners list the tickets they already have and those they want.

⚠
The woman says that she is looking forward to the women's marathon, but it is not clear whether she has tickets for this event.

CD 1/31
See the tapescript on p. 190 of the Learner's Book.

2b) Key
They already have tickets for:
gymnastics, archery, rowing

They would like to get tickets for:
beach volleyball, badminton, wrestling, swimming

2c)

There are, of course, many more Olympic sports. Learners now work in pairs or groups of three and write down as many other Olympic sports, for both summer and winter games, as they can think of. They can use their dictionaries for this activity.

When they have had sufficient time to complete their lists, collect their contributions on the board.

➡ Olympic sports

Summer sports not listed in 2a) include:
baseball; basketball; boxing; canoe/kayak; cycling; fencing; football; handball; judo; modern pentathlon; sailing; shooting; softball; table tennis; Taekwondo; tennis; triathlon; weightlifting.

Winter sports include:
biathlon; bobsleigh; curling; ice hockey; luge; skating; skiing

2c) Key
Learners' own contributions

2d)

Now ask learners to look at the language in the box. Can they think of any other verbs that could be used to express like/dislike (e.g. *love, enjoy, can't stand*)?

Using this language, learners work in pairs and talk about the sports they enjoy watching.

3a)

Before learners begin this activity, discuss the topic of weblogs. Has anyone in the group ever kept one? If so, for what purpose? What might be the advantages/disadvantages of keeping a weblog rather than a more traditional form of diary when on holiday?

➡ weblog (usually shortened to 'blog')
A personal journal or on-line diary, often in the form of a scrapbook including photos or other images.

Learners first read the questions on p. 57, then look at the three weblog entries on p. 58, which document the events of the first three days in Athens. Note that Days 1 and 3 are written by Beth whereas Day 2 is by Dan.

Learners then read the texts for detail, numbering the boxes according to whether the situation took place on Day 1, 2 or 3. Ask learners to underline the information as they find it in the weblog and read out the corresponding text segment when they give their answers.

3a) Key
1. Day 3
2. Day 1
3. Day 1
4. Day 2
5. Day 3
6. Day 2

3b)

Learners now reread the entries for more detail. This time, they decide whether the statements are true or false. Again, ask them to underline the segment in the text that confirms their choice.

Ignore the Grammar box for the moment. It is probably best dealt with in 4b).

3b) Key
True: 2, 5, 6
False: 1, 3, 4, 7, 8

4a)

Learners were introduced to relative clauses in Unit 4 of Fairway 2. Here they deal for the first time with Defining relative clauses. (Non-defining relative clauses are dealt with in Unit 6.)

Ask learners to read the sentences in 4a) and circle the correct relative pronoun.

➡ Relative clauses
- A defining relative clause is essential to the sense of the sentence, e.g.
  The man <u>who invented the modern Olympic Games</u> was Baron de Coubertin.
- A non-defining relative clause provides additional information and can be dropped from the sentence without affecting the overall meaning, e.g.
  The inventor of the modern Olympic Games, <u>which first took place in 1896</u>, was Baron de Coubertin.

⚠ commas in relative clauses
Whereas in German all relative clauses are indicated by a preceding comma, in English commas are only necessary in the case of non-defining relative clauses (see the examples above in the note above).

4a) Key
Sentences:
1. who, 2. that, 3. which, 4. who, 5. that, 6. that, 7. that, 8. who

4b)

Now ask learners to look at the information in the Grammar box and complete the sentence below it. They then look through the sentences in 4a) again. This time they underline the relative pronouns that can be left out.

4b) Key
Grammar box:
zusammenstehen

No pronoun required:
3, 5, 6, 7

4c)

Learners now practise using defining relative clauses. First, ask them to read the eight topics. What characterises each of the statements? (All contain relative clauses but the relative pronoun has been left out.) Elicit the meaning of each of the sentences.

Ask learners to look at the prompt box, which focuses on relative clauses. They then form groups of three, choose one of the topics and talk about it, using defining relative clauses as often as possible.

4d)

Learners now try to use the new structure accurately in written form. Ask them to look at the statements in 4a) and choose one they would like to expand. They can, of course, amend the statement to suit their circumstances, e.g. *Paris is one of the nicest places I've visited.*

Remind learners that the use of the relative pronoun is always correct. If uncertain, they should leave it in. Given time and more exposure to the structure, learners will develop a feel for when to use it and when it can be dropped.

You might want to collect these texts and check whether learners have grasped this new structure. Return them corrected and give general feedback using examples from the learners' texts.

TIPP für erfolgreiche Kommunikation
Much of Unit 5 is devoted to reporting, and this TIPP covers some of the basics of good reporting. Some very useful discourse markers are featured here. Discourse markers help to maintain the context in which the discourse is taking place by orienting the listener to the speaker's main intentions. There are various types of discourse marker; in this section we are dealing with 'adjuncts', which provide the content focus or give personal perspective on the part of the speaker.

Ask learners to look at the extracts featuring the adjuncts, which are all placed at the beginning of the sentence:

*… **so** I went …*
***Well**, Mr Stavros told us …*
***Anyway**, the big news is …*
***However**, the latest surveys suggest …*

What purpose does each one serve? They make the report flow more smoothly, but each in a slightly different way. Elicit these differences from the learners, if possible.

*… **so** / **well**, …:*
These keep a narrative flowing smoothly without shifting the focus from the content.

***Anyway**, …*
This signals the end of one phase of the report and the start of another.

***However**, …*
This opens a new aspect in the topic.

***Unfortunately**; …*
This functions a bit differently, in that it indicates the speaker's personal perspective.

Ask learners to read the remaining information in the TIPP box, then ask them to look back at the weblog. Assign each pair of learners one of the three days. Ask them to read through their text and decide whether it is an example of good reporting. What features make it good? Have the ideas presented in the TIPP been integrated into the text?

New Zealand

Unit summary

This unit features New Zealand and highlights various aspects of its culture, history, wildlife, climate and geography. The grammar sections focus on non-defining relative clauses and *if*-clauses. The pronunciation activity focuses on intonation in non-defining relative clauses. Learners create a tourist ad for their country or city. They also write a poem using eleven words.

Part A: This bird, which can't fly, is the national symbol

Focus
Quiz about New Zealand
Interesting aspects of New Zealand and its people
Tourist ad for one's own country

Grammar
Non-defining relative clauses: *This bird, which can't fly, is the national symbol.*

Pronunciation
Intonation:
Sentences that include Non-defining relative clauses

1a) Revision: relative pronouns *who, which, whose*

New Zealand is a place many people would love to visit and it is becoming increasingly popular as a holiday destination. Ask if anyone has been to the country. If so, ask them to say what particularly impressed them. Then, brainstorm words or phrases that learners associate with New Zealand. The large picture on p. 62 (which shows Mount Cook) might give them some ideas. Gather them on the board.

Now ask learners to look at the quiz and complete the sentences with the relative pronouns supplied in the instruction.

1a) Key

1. who, 2. which, 3. which, 4. who, 5. whose, 6. which

1b)

Learners now work in groups of three and answer the questions. Unless they just happen to know something about New Zealand, there will probably be a good bit of speculating in the groups, which is fine. This uncertainty will motivate them to listen more intently to the recording.

1b) Key

1. Captain James Cook
2. Christchurch
3. rugby
4. Maori
5. Great Britain
6. English and Maori

1c)

Tell learners they will hear two people talking about a quiz while sitting on a plane on the way to New Zealand. A man is quizzing a woman who is not the least interested in what he is saying.

Play the recording and learners check their answers.

➡ Flag of New Zealand

The flag of New Zealand has the British flag – the 'Union Jack' – in the upper left-hand quarter. The remaining three-quarters of the flag are dark blue. On the right-hand side is a design of red stars with white borders, ordered like a cross. The stars represent the constellation of Crux, the Southern Cross, as seen from New Zealand.

➡ Captain James Cook (1728-1779)

Cook was an English explorer, navigator and cartographer. His most notable accomplishments were the British discovery and claiming of the east coast of Australia; the European discovery of the Hawaiian Islands; and the first recorded circumnavigation and mapping of Newfoundland and New Zealand. The ship on his first great voyage was named 'Endeavour'; this later lent its name to the space shuttle 'Endeavour'. Cook was killed and probably eaten by the natives of Hawaii. Although Hawaii has been a state of the USA since 1898, its flag also still has the British Union Jack in its top left-hand quarter.

CD 1/32

See the tapescript on p. 190 of the Learner's Book.

2a)

These texts include many interesting facts about New Zealand. Ask learners to first look at the words in the exercise at the bottom of the page on the left, then skim the text and match the words with the English definitions. They should ignore the words in the text that are underlined for the moment.

➡ Pronouncing the Maori words

tawa ['tæwə]
kakapo ['kækəpəʊ]
Pakeha ['pækehʌ]

➥ bungee jumping

The first known example of this popular sport occurred on April Fool's Day (April 1) 1979, when members of the Oxford University Dangerous Sports Club jumped from Bristol Suspension Bridge. The sport was quickly popularised and commercialised in New Zealand. 'Bunjee' is an old slang word for rubber/eraser, and may come from a Hindu word meaning 'elastic'.

2a) Key

1a, 2c, 3d, 4e, 5a

1. bungee jumping – an adventure sport
2. tawa – a tree
3. kakapo – a type of bird
4. Pakeha – a race of people
5. Haka – a war dance

2b)

Ask learners to read the six statements, then read the text again and mark the statements true or false. They should underline the segment of the text which confirms their choice.

2b) Key

True: 2, 3, 6
False: 1, 4, 5

2c)

Learners read the text once more, this time focusing their attention on the words which are underlined and matching them with the synonyms in 2c). Let them do this without any help from you. Although some of the words may be unfamiliar, they should be able to deduce the meanings from the context.

When they have finished, ask various learners to give their answers. Check that their pronunciation of any important new words (e.g. *villages, mountainous, spectacular*) is correct.

2c) Key

stories – tales
villages / small towns – settlements
places to find natural water – springs
uncommon / not many left – rare
mountainous and wild – rugged
something very exciting – thrill
very beautiful and spectacular – stunning
far away from other places – isolated

3a)

Ask learners to focus their attention on the Grammar box, which features non-defining relative clauses and includes two types of example.

- In the first example the relative clause is attached to the end of a complete sentence:
  There you will find the wonderful Southern Alps, ***which go from the north to the south of the island.***
- In the remaining examples the relative clause is inserted into a complete sentence:
  This brown bird, ***which can't fly,*** *is the national symbol of New Zealand.*

Ask learners to read through the examples. Is the information in the clauses is essential to the sentence? If it were left out, would the meaning of the sentence still be perfectly clear? (Yes, it would; non-defining relative clauses only add information. What is the function of the commas? (They separate the relative clause from the rest of the sentence.)

⚠ Commas

Note that removing commas from a sentence can change the meaning completely:

- *The springs, which are a mile up the road, are very popular for swimming.*

(There is one set of springs.)

- *The springs which are a mile up the road are very popular for swimming.*

(There are several springs. Of those, the ones up the road a mile are popular.)

Now ask learners to look at the sentences in 3a). In each example there are two sentences which can be condensed into one by using a non-defining relative clause. Once they have written their sentence, they can check it by leaving out the non-defining clause. Does the sentence still contain the essential information? Ask learners to look at the first example, and check it by leaving out the clause, e.g. *Edmund Hillary … was the first man to climb Mount Everest.*

Learners work individually and join the sentences. Check by asking learners to come forward and write their sentences on the board. Make certain the commas have been placed correctly. Note that in some cases the sentence can also be assembled differently (see the key below).

3a) Key

1. Edmund Hillary, who was born in New Zealand, was the first man to climb Mount Everest.
2. Mount Cook, which is 3,754m high, is the highest mountain in New Zealand.
3. Te Awamutu, which is a Maori word, is the name of a town in New Zealand.
4. The kea, which is an unusual looking bird, is only found on the South Island of New Zealand.
5. Captain James Cook, whose ship was called 'The Endeavour', claimed the islands for Great Britain in 1769.

6. Peter Jackson, who directed the 'Lord of the Rings' films, was born in 1961.
7. 80% of New Zealand's population, which is around 4 million, lives in cities.

Also possible:

1. Edmund Hillary, who was the first man to climb Mount Everest, was born in New Zealand.
2. Mount Cook, which is the highest mountain in New Zealand, is 3,754m high.
3. Te Awamutu, which is the name of a town in New Zealand, is a Maori word.
4. The kea, which is only found on the South Island of New Zealand, is an unusual looking bird.
6. Peter Jackson, who was born in 1961, directed the 'Lord of the Rings' films.

3b)

In this exercise learners practise sentences containing non-defining clauses. The commas which separate non-defining clauses from the main clause signal a break in the flow of speech, thus audibly separating the non-defining clause from the main clause. In addition to this, the non-defining clause is spoken with a noticeable fall in pitch.

Play the recording, stopping after each sentence for learners to repeat.

CD 1/33
See the sentences in 3b).

3c)

Learners now personalise the structure they have just learnt and talk about family and friends with each other. Ask them to look at the prompt box, which again features non-defining relative clauses. Then tell learners to think of five people they would like to describe. Each of the descriptions should include a non-defining relative clause.

Learners work together in groups of four and take it in turns to tell about friends and family members they have chosen.

4a)

In this activity, learners work in groups of three or four and write an ad about an aspect of their country or area that would attract tourists. First, they decide on the aspect they would like to focus on, then decide who they want to attract, why they think their chosen aspect will interest people, and, finally, how they want to attract them.

After reaching agreement about their ad, they should decide on the text for it, then write it up appropriately. A group secretary could be designated to write the end product.

4b)

One person from each group reads their ad to the class. Learners then vote on the best one.

Part B: If it rains, I won't go

Focus
Seasons, climate and geography of New Zealand
Song, 'Raining in My Heart', by Leo Sayer
Poems with eleven words

Grammar
Conditional 1: *If*+ Present simple tense + *will* future (Revision)

Functions
Expressing displeasure: *Stop it, Bill!*
Criticising: *Don't be silly, Jenny.*
Expressing disinterest: *Who cares about ...?*
Giving the source of some information: *According to (the forecast).*

1 Revision: non-defining relative clauses

In this exercise learners play the role of a tourist guide, describing different areas of their country. They should talk about the location, the geography and the temperatures of the area and use a non-defining clause when doing so. The prompt box will give them a clear example of how they can start their descriptions.

Carry this out as a group activity, calling on learners to make individual statements.

2a)

As New Zealand is in the Southern Hemisphere, learners will have to think for a moment before filling in the seasons. Pronounce the example, *autumn*, and ask learners to repeat after you. Learners then fill in the remaining ones.

2a) Key
September-December: spring
December-March: summer
March-June: autumn
June-September: winter

2b)

Play the recording and learners check their answers.

CD 1/34
See the tapescript on p. 190 of the Learner's Book.

2c)

Ask learners to look at the list of adjectives describing temperatures. What temperatures would they themselves consider to be *mild*, *warm* or *cool*? Then ask them to read the short text on the climate in New Zealand and write the words in the correct spaces.

After the reading, elicit the meaning of *temperate*. Where would they put *hot* and *cold* on this scale?

2c) Key
warm, mild, cool, freezing

2d)

In this activity learners give a mini-presentation. They should reckon to speak for 15 to 30 seconds.

Ask learners to think about which of the four seasons they like best. Then ask them to make notes about why it is their favourite season and what they particularly enjoy doing during that time of the year. The prompt box will help them structure their ideas.

When they have had sufficient time to write down their ideas and decide what they wish to say, ask them to take it in turns to give their presentations. They should try to speak freely and not read from a prepared text.

2d) Key
Learners' own presentations

3a)

Ask learners to look at the list of words and pronounce them. Most of them are so similar in German that learners should have no problems matching them with the pictures.

3a) Key
1. windy, 2. foggy, 3. raining, 4. sunny, 5. cloudy, 6. snowing

3b)

Learners now work in pairs and take it in turns to be tourist guides. They tell each other as much as they can about the weather in various areas of their own country. The prompt box at the top of p. 68 will help them structure their statements. They should use adverbs of frequency in their descriptions.

4a)

Ask learners to look at the map of New Zealand. What information can be gleaned from it? (size and shape of the islands; location of cities; location of the capital, Wellington; topography, etc.)

Now, learners listen to the weather forecast for Wellington and decide what season it might be.

CD 1/35
See the tapescript on pp. 190-191 of the Learner's Book.

4a) Key
Spring or autumn

4b)

Learners listen to the recording again and note the weather over the next few days.

4b) Key
this morning: mild, 9/10°
this afternoon: rainy
this evening: rainy, cooler (just over 5°; possibly storms in Auckland)
tomorrow: warmer but cloudy
the weekend: nice and warm, but windy

5a)

Ask learners to cover the dialogue on the right-hand side of the page. Tell them they will hear three people discussing their plans for the day. Then ask them to read the four questions.

Play the recording and learners answer the questions. (Jenny is the third speaker on the recording.)

CD 1/36
See the dialogue in 5b) and the key to 5b).

5a) Key
1. Wellington
2. He wants to go to the beach.
3. No, he doesn't like shopping.
4. She wants to go bungee jumping.

5b)

Now ask learners to look at the dialogue and the words under the picture. Working individually learners fill in the words in the correct places.

5b) Key
1. Who cares
2. could be
3. it rains
4. according to
5. won't go
6. you go

5c)

Play the recording and learners check their answers.

5d)

Learners work in groups of three and practise the dialogue. Remind them that each should play all the roles. Ask them to put emotion into the dialogue and really bring it to life.

Now, ask learners to look at the information in the Grammar box. The two example sentences have been taken from the dialogue. Ask learners to go back to the dialogue and read these two sentences in context. How likely is it that it will rain? (The weather forecast predicts rain, so in all probability it will rain.)

Now, ask learners to look at the main clause. Which tense is used here? (Future simple)

What else could be noted about the *if*-clauses? When the *if*-clause is at the beginning of a sentence, it is separated from the main clause by a comma. When it is at the end of the sentence, there is no comma.

Learners now fill in the text with the missing word.

5d) Key
Grammar box:
wahrscheinlich

6a)

In this activity learners work with a choice of *if*-clauses and main clauses and create sensible sentences using the two elements.

Learners work in pairs and take it in turn to create sentences using the elements from the list. The partner comments on whether the sentence is sensible or not, then makes another sentence using other elements from the list.

6a) Key
Learners' own sentences

6b)

After learners have created a number of sentences, they tell each other which of their own sentences are true, or nearly true, for themselves. If they choose, they can amend the phrases slightly to make them true, e.g. *If we have enough time, we'll go to Vienna next month.*

6c)

In this activity learners use *if-* clauses to create their own sentences, saying what they will do at specific times and under specific weather conditions. The language in the prompt box will help them get started.

Before they walk around and talk to others, they should write the times in the list onto a slip of paper. When talking to people, they should try to mention two of these times.

Learners walk around and talk to each other about their plans. To keep the activity moving quickly, they should make one set of statements, listen to the partner's set of statements, then move on to someone else.

You might like to introduce the phrase, *How about you?*, which would make the turn-taking more natural.

6c) Key
Learners' own sentences

7a)

Ask learners to cover the song with a piece of paper. Write the title, 'Raining in My Heart' on the board. Ask learners to speculate as to what might be coming up in the lyrics. Why is it raining in the singer's heart?

Finally, ask learners to read the text and fill in the missing words with words they think are suitable.

➡ **Leo Sayer**
Gerard Hugh Sayer is an English singer, recording artist and song writer who has had a long career, with successful singles such as the 'The Show Must Go On' dating from 1973 to the present. He was given the name Leo because of his lion-like mane of curly hair.

7a) Key
1. blue, 2. cloud, 3. today, 4. know, 5. blues, 6. tears, 7. blue, 8. cloud

7b)

Play the song and learners check their answers.

Focus on the phrase *my blues won't show*. Do learners know what this means? The expression *to have the blues*, or *to feel blue* is based on the type of music called *the blues*, in which songs often are about difficulties or bad luck.

Have learners come across any other way in which the word *blue* is used in English?

Some expressions:
- *to be blue with cold*
- *to happen out of the blue* (= to happen very unexpectedly)
- *to happen once in a blue moon* (= to happen very rarely)
- *a blue movie* (= a film that shows expicit sex)

How is the word *blue* used in the learners' own language? Does it have meanings that are completely different? (*blau* = *inebriated, drunk*)

CD 1/37
See the tapescript on p. 191 of the Learner's Book.

8

In this writing activity, learners create a poem of eleven words. Point out that the word *poem* in this context has little to do with the poetry from their school days. In this activity, learners simply play with words and create something of their own.

The rules are simple: the first line has one word, the second has two words, the third three words, the fourth, four words and the last line again only one word. The subject is entirely up to the learners.

Learners should write their poem on a separate sheet of paper. Give them about five minutes for the task. Gather the poems and lay them out on a table or hang them on the wall. Learners can walk around and look at each others' poems.

Ambition

Unit summary

This unit focuses on dreams and plans for the future. The new grammar is Conditional 2, together with future possibility using *might, probably* and *definitely*. Verbs with *to* + infinitive are revised. The pronunciation section contrasts *I* and *I'd*. The *TIPP für erfolgreiche Kommunikation* features various aspects of small talk and persuading.

Part A: I might sail around the world

Focus
Long term goals and dreams
Plans for the weekend

Functions
Expressing degree of certainty: *We'll probably go to Europe …; I probably won't ever …; I might get to see (Paris); I'll definitely (plant a tree).*
Retracting a statement: *No, that's a lie.*
Recommending something: *You should go; That's really something you should try and see.*
Expressing hopes: *I hope to see …; I'd love to go… one day.*
Expressing regret: *Unfortunately not.*
Making excuses: *The problem's time; Life's too short.*
Encouraging someone to do something: *So do it.*
Keeping options open: *We haven't made any definite plans yet, but …*

Grammar
Conditional 1 (Revision): *If I give up my job, I'll have more free time.*
Verbs with *to* + infinitive (Revision): *I want to/hope to …; I'd love to / like to …*
Future possibilities (Revision): *might, probably, definitely*

1a) Revision: Conditional 1

In these sentences learners create a chain of statements, each of which is dependent on conditions described in the foregoing statement.

Ask learners to look at the first example and elicit the features of the structure (*if* +Present simple, and *will* in the main clause). Working individually, they then write sentences using the phrases given.

1a) Key
1. If I give up my job, I'll have more free time.
2. If I have enough time, I'll write a novel.
3. If my book is a success, I'll make a lot of money.
4. If I become rich, I'll buy a house by the sea.
5. If I live by the sea, I'll get lots of ideas.
6. If I get good ideas, I'll write more books.
7. If I write more books, I'll become really famous.

1b)

Learners now personalise the structure and write five or six sentences about things they will do at a weekend in their favourite town or city. The language in the prompt box should be used as a model.

1c)

When learners have finished their sentences, ask them to work in groups of three and exchange ideas.

2a)

Ask learners to look at the magazine extract at the top of p. 75. What city is Tina working in? (Vancouver, Canada) Perhaps someone in your group has visited this beautiful city and can tell the group something about it.

Ask learners to look at the list of verbs, then read the text. Learners now complete the phrases by filling in the appropriate verb. Point out that the verb *go* occurs twice in the list.

➡ Vancouver
Vancouver is located in western Canada in the province of British Columbia. The city itself has a population of around 600,000, while that of the metropolitan area is around 2,000,000. Vancouver ranks in the top five in world-wide rankings for quality of life. It is renowned for its beautiful scenery. The city itself has one of North America's largest urban parks, Stanley Park. The beautiful island of the same name, Vancouver Island, is located across the Strait of Georgia, a body of water which shields Vancouver from the Pacific.

➡ Mount Logan
Canada's highest peak (5,959m), is located in the Saint Elias Range in the Yukon Territory. It is the second highest peak in North America, the highest being Denali (6,194 m) in Alaska.

➡ Stanley Cup
This is the championship trophy of the National Hockey League. It is a prize with a long history: the first play-offs for the cup were held in March, 1894.

2a) Key
1. write, 2. climb, 3. see, 4. learn, 5. run, 6. plant, 7. visit, 8. go, 9. go, 10. spend

2b)

Ask learners to look at the language in the prompt box. Which tense is used to describe these experiences? Why is the Present perfect used here? (These are things that still might happen, although they haven't happened yet.)

Here learners use the ideas in 2a) as a springboard to talk about their own experiences. Certainly they won't have done many of the things in the list, but they can talk about comparable experiences of their own.

Working individually, learners think of some memorable personal experiences, then compare with a partner. Finish by asking them to report one thing they learned about their partner.

3a)

Tell learners they will hear two women talking about the article in 2a), then ask them to read the two questions. Play the recording, then check.

CD 2/2
See the tapescript on p. 191 of the Learner's Book.

3a) Key
1. Both women are forty.
2. Sandy has visited Paris, run a marathon (and written the first page of a bestseller!).

3b)

Tell learners they will hear a continuation of the recording. The other speaker, Cathy, now talks about what she has done and what she would like to do.

Ask learners to read the language in the speech bubble and elicit the meaning of the sentence. Learners complete the dialogue using the phrases supplied.

3b) Key
1. scared of heights
2. wanted to do
3. I'll have more time.
4. made any definite plans
5. That would be fantastic
6. Life's just too short.

3c)

Play the recording and learners check their answers.

CD 2/3
See the dialogue in 3b) and the key to 3b).

3d)

Learners now work in pairs and practise the dialogue.

4a)

Ask learners to look at the Grammar box, which features ways of expressing future possibilities. Ask them to read the examples, then focus their attention on the words expressing degree of possibility, e.g. *might, probably, definitely*. Which of these expresses the greatest/least degree of likelihood? (*definitely/might*)

Learners now talk to a partner about the things in the list in 2a), saying how likely it is that they will do them at some point in their own lives.

4b)

Learners now think for a moment about their goals and plans for the next twelve months, then write down one statement for each of the four options.

4c)

Learners now talk to a partner about their plans. Ask them to report one thing their partner told them.

5a)

Tell learners they will hear a radio interview with two people talking about their ambitions and dreams. First, ask learners to look at the pictures and read the speech bubbles. Elicit the meaning of the statements. What structure characterises both statements? (verb *to* + infinitive)

CD 2/4
See the tapescript on p. 191 of the Learners' Book.

5a) Key
Sue Lee:
She'd love to spend a few months in China and she wants to see the Wall.

Trevor James:
He hopes to win Wimbledon.
He would like to turn professional when he finishes school and he hopes to play on the ATP tour.

5b)

Learners work with a partner and compare notes. If there are any discrepancies, play the recording again for checking purposes.

Ask learners to look at the Grammar box, which features a revision of verbs requiring *to* + infinitive.

5c)

Learners now personalise the language, using the verbs *want to, like to*, and *hope to* to talk about things they plan to do before they are eighty.

Ask each person to make a list of five things on a slip of paper.

5d)

When learners have finished their lists, ask them to walk around and exchange ideas with others in the group. If they find someone with the same ideas, they should note this down.

Gather feedback. Learners report on others who have the same things on their list.

Part B: If I wasn't scared of heights, I'd go

Focus
A visit to Vancouver
How adventurous are you? – Questionnaire

Functions
Expressing surprise: *I can hardly believe (I'm leaving on Friday).*
Expressing regret: *It's a pity …; Yes, it's a shame.*
Asking for a suggestion: *What would you like to do today?*
Suggesting: *What do you suggest?; I know! (Capilano!)*
Declining: *Oh no. I don't think so, thanks.; I wouldn't (walk over that bridge) if you paid me.*
Persuading: *We could just (go and look); Oh, Come on! You're usually so adventurous.*

Grammar
Conditional 2: *If you were here for another week, I'd take you to …*

Pronunciation
Sounds:
You like it / You'd like it.

What you need
Unit 7B, 4a): Dictionaries for individual work.

1a) Revision: expressing probability using *definitely, might, probably (won't)*

Ask the class to look at the picture and describe the man in the foreground (George Graham). Does he appear to be fit and active? Is he friendly, outgoing? How old might he be? Is he wealthy? Is he on holiday?

Ask learners to look at the language in the prompt box, then at the list of activities and decide which of them he might do during his two-week visit to Vancouver. They should try to use phrases of confirmation and connecting phrases when talking to each other, e.g. *That's right; And …*

1b)

George Graham is talking to someone on his mobile while waiting for his daughter to fetch him at the airport. During the conversation he mentions a number of things he might or might not do during his visit.

Learners listen to the recording to find out which two things from the list in 1a) George does not mention. Suggest that learners tick the items they hear and see what is left over. Make certain learners understand that the items only need to be mentioned; it is irrelevant whether George intends to do them or not.

Play the recording and learners decide which two things he does not mention.

CD 2/5
See the tapescript on p. 192 of the Learner's Book.

1b) Key
He doesn't mention:
– cycle in the park,
– go shopping for presents.

2a)

Ask learners to look at the picture and describe the situation.

Then, ask them to focus their attention on the speech bubbles. Elicit the meanings of the sentences. Learners are familiar with the first conditional (*if*-clause + *will* in the main clause), which expresses probability. Ask them to examine the tenses in these examples more closely. Which tense is used in the *if*-clause? (Past simple). Which form is used in the main clause? (*I'd = I would*). How likely is it that these things will happen? (very unlikely).

Learners now look at the questions. Play the recording, using the pause button to allow them sufficient time to fill in the answers. If necessary, play the recording a second time.

CD 2/6
See the dialogue in 2b) and the key to 2b).

2a) Key
1. He's going home in two days/on Friday.
2. There isn't enough time.
3. It's made of wood and rope.
4. He's scared of heights.
5. He wants to go shopping and have a cup of tea.

2b)

Working individually, learners read the dialogue and mark the correct options.

2b) Key
1. days; 2. I'd take; 3. would; 4. time; 5. suggest;
6. I wasn't scared; 7. paid me; 8. adventurous

2c)

Play the recording and learners check their answers. Make certain they discriminate between *I* and *I'd*. This is often a source of confusion; the difference between the two words can make a crucial difference. Step 3a), which focuses on pronunciation, offers additional practice.

2d)

Working in pairs, learners practise the dialogue. The learner who plays Janet should try to be enthusiastic about her suggestion and as convincing as possible.

Get learners to look at the Grammar box, which presents the second conditional. Ask them to read the examples, then complete the sentence below the box.

2d) Key
Grammar box:
unwahrscheinlich

3a)

Just as it is not always easy to hear the difference between *I* and *I'll*, so learners often have difficulty in distinguishing between *I* and *I'd*.

Ask them to look at the sentences and practise reading them to each other in pairs. Play the recording while they mark the sentences they hear.

3a) Key + CD 2/7
1. I'd eat it; 2. You like it; 3. I'd take it; 4. I go there.

3b)

Play the recording, stopping after each example. Ask learners to repeat it before moving on to the next sentence.

CD 2/8
See the sentences in 3b).

4a)

In this step learners personalise the second conditional. Give them plenty of time for this and let them use a dictionary if necessary.

4b)

The statements written in 4a) are of a personal nature and most learners will probably be interested in finding out what the others have written.

Ask someone to read out one of their sentences. Then, go round the class asking others to say how they completed the same statement. When everyone has had a turn, ask another learner to read another statement, then call on others to read out their versions, and so on.

Personal information makes this activity interesting, but its main purpose is to use the second conditional accurately. So, correct any mistakes in usage as the exercise progresses.

5a)

Ask learners to look at the magazine questionnaire. The picture shows the Capilano Bridge that was mentioned in 2b). How many people in the class are adventurous enough to want to cross this bridge?

Working individually, learners now read the questionnaire and answer the questions. When they have finished, they should work out their scores.

➡ **Get a life!**
This idiomatic expression means 'Do something more interesting or exciting with your time!'

5b)

Ask learners to look at the language in the first box. Then, ask someone to read A. Read the B part yourself. It is important that learners note the stress on <u>*Would*</u> *you?* Were it intended to be a real question, the stress would be on <u>*you*</u>. In this context, it is not a real question, but rather an expression of surprise or disbelief.

6a)

Learners now work in pairs and add to the questionnaire. Each pair writes two additional questions with three answers to choose from, as in the questionnaire. They also decide on the number of points they want to award to each answer. Each person writes down the two questions and the choices on a piece of paper.

6b)

The pairs now split up. Each learner asks someone else his/her additional questions. They then exchange their questions, and go on to do the same with another person. Let the exercise carry on until learners have exchanged questions a few times.

Tipp für erfolgreiche Kommunikation
The information in this block sums up important strategies and functional language for 'small talk' and for persuading someone to do something, or declining something that has been suggested. Ask learners to read the information.

Ask them whether they think the register is formal or informal. Would they use this language with people they don't know well, or would they use it in informal situations with people they know well?

➡ **register**
The style of language that we use in different situations, e.g. with a small child, an old friend, an employer, etc.

The dialogue in 1b) presents much of this useful language in a natural situation. Ask learners to read the dialogue again and mark the functional language they find there. Then ask them to choose their favourite phrase and compare their choice with a partner.

Feelings

Unit summary

The unit centres around moods, emotions and ways of expressing them. Learners work mainly with mini-dialogues covering a wide variety of situations with emotional content. The new grammar features are possessive pronouns and the Past Perfect tense. There is also a reading text on the use of colours in home decoration.

Part A: It's always been a dream of hers

Focus
Body language and facial expression
Expressing feelings
Personal news
Use of colour in the home

Functions
Commenting on someone's mood: *What are you so happy about?; You're in a good mood; What's the matter with you?; What are you so bothered about?*
Expressing pleasure: *That's great news.; Fantastic.*
Congratulating someone: *Congratulations!; She really deserves it; Good for her; Well done.*
Expressing sympathy: *Sorry to hear that.*
Wishing someone well: *I'm sure you'll do better next time; Better luck next time.*
Expressing disappointment: *That's easy for you to say.; I think I could have done better.*
Calming someone: *Calm down!; Don't get so angry about it; Take it easy.*

Grammar
Possessive pronouns: *You can borrow mine; It's a dream of ours*, etc.

Pronunciation
Intonation when expressing emotions:
Congratulations; That's great news; Calm down; etc.

1a) Revision: general vocabulary; dictionary use

Everyone has very special things that make them happy: activities, events, special people, thoughts, etc.

In this activity learners work individually and write down a variety of things that make them feel happy. They can use a dictionary for this. They should write their lists on a separate piece of paper.

Walk around during the activity and help out with vocabulary, if necessary.

1a) Key
Learners' own statements

1b)

Ask learners to look at the prompt box, which features two different ways of expressing what makes one happy. Ask a few learners to use one of these structures and mention one thing that makes them feel happy.

Then, ask learners to stand up and walk around with their lists and compare their ideas with others.

1c)

Elicit the meaning of good/bad mood. Ask learners to look at the various pictures, each of which depicts a mood through the use of typical body language and facial expression. Pronounce each of the words and ask learners to repeat after you. Elicit the meaning of each.

Ask learners to look at the pictures. Do they think the facial expressions and body language shown here are universal?. Would other expressions and gestures be used in their culture to express the same feelings?

➡ Facial Expression and body Language
The significance of facial expression and body language in communication are topics which have been researched in depth over the past few decades, bringing interesting information to light.

Studies of blind and deaf people indicate that much unconscious body language and facial expression is inborn and universal. Studies indicate that about two thirds of a message in face-to-face communication is non-verbal. Gesture, on the other hand, gesture is learned and varies from culture to culture.

For a more detailed study on this topic, see:
Russell, J.A. and Fernandez-Dols, Jose Miqual, eds. The Psychology of Facial Expression (Studies in Emotion and Social Interaction). Cambridge University Press. ISBN: 0521587964.

1c) Key
Learners' own statements

1d)

Tell learners they are now going to hear short utterances made by people in very particular moods. Learners listen to each of the utterances, then decide how the speaker is feeling.

Play the recording, stopping after each speaker. Gather opinions from learners before moving on to the next utterance. What, besides the text itself, gives us the clues?

CD 2/9
See the tapescript on p. 192 of the Learner's Book.

1d) Key

Woman 1:	upset
Man 1:	bored
Woman 2:	disappointed
Man 2:	nervous
Woman 3:	angry
Man 3:	excited.

1e)

As learners to look at the questions in the list and discuss the questions with a partner. Remind them to ask each other the questions using the phrase *How would you feel if…*+ the Past simple tense.

1e) Key
Learners' own statements

1f)

Learners now work individually and think of three other situations and write them down. Again, they work in pairs and ask each other how they would feel in the given situations.

1f) Key
Learners' own statements

2a)

This step consists of five mini-dialogues, each of which contains very useful functional language. Each situation illustrates a particular mood and presents phrases for dealing adequately with each of the situations. Encourage learners to practise the dialogues until they come naturally.

Work through the dialogues individually. Learners read them, then decide which feeling person B and person D are expressing. Using the language in the box, learners give their opinions.

2a) Key
Dialogue 1: Person B is really happy.
Dialogue 2: Person D is really disappointed.
Dialogue 3: Person D is angry.
Dialogue 4: Person B is happy.
Dialogue 5: Person D is excited.

2b)

Ask learners to look at the phrases below the instructions. Each of these can be used to replace one of the phrases underlined in the dialogues in 2a). Read each of the phrases and ask learners to repeat them after you. When you read them, show emotion and exaggerate the intonation a bit so that learners get a feel for the phrases.

Learners then work individually and match up the phrases from the list with those underlined in the dialogue.

2b) Key
Dialogue 1: Good for her.
Dialogue 2: Better luck next time.
Dialogue 3: Take it easy.
Dialogue 4: Fantastic.
Dialogue 5: Well done.

2c)

Play the dialogue and learners check their answers.

CD 2/10
See the dialogues on p. 192 of the Learner's Book.

2d)

Ask learners to look at the dialogues in 2a) again and read the first line of each one. Call on various learners to read individual ones, putting emotion into it. Listen for appropriate intonation; this is a very important feature of this type of language.

Learners then work in pairs. Using only the first line of the mini-dialogues, they create their own dialogue. They should use the expressions as often as they can.

3a)

In this activity, learners practise intonation once more. Play the utterances, stopping between each one for learners to practise. Give each learner an opportunity to practise individually. Ask them to really show emotion when it's their turn to repeat the phrase.

CD 2/11
See the five phrases in 3a).

3b)
Learners now personalise the language they have been practising. Ask them to look at the prompt box at the top of p. 86.

Each person then invents four pieces of personal news, both good and bad. Working in pairs, they take it in turns to tell each other their news. The partner responds appropriately, using as much of the new language as possible.

3b) Key
Learners' own statements

4

Ask learners to direct their attention to the Grammar in the box, which features possessive pronouns. Ask them to read the example sentences. Elicit the function of the possessive pronouns in each sentence, i.e. they replace another noun which has already been mentioned in the context.

Point out that the use of possessive pronouns is not difficult if one has learned the proper forms. This is more a point of lexical rather than conceptual grammar. Be prepared for German learners to come up with sentences such as *He is a friend of us*.

Working individually, learners complete the dialogues with the correct possessive pronoun.

4 Key
1. mine, 2. theirs, 3. mine, 4. yours, 5. Ours, 6. his

5

The reading text is about colours, moods and home decoration. Learners read the text and put the colours into two groups, good ones and bad ones. They should also note which colours are good/bad for the different rooms, as some colours are good for some rooms, whereas they are bad for others.

Discuss the ideas with your group. How colourful are their own homes? Do they agree with the text? Do they enjoy living with different colours on the walls or do they prefer neutral walls, adding colour with furniture, curtains, rugs, pictures, etc?

5 Key
Good colours:
red for the bathroom
green for the living room or bedroom, also the study
yellow for the kitchen and dining room
blue for the bedroom
grey for a bathroom that teenagers spend too much time in

Bad colours:
red for the dining room
blue for living room or kitchen
grey for most of the house

Part B: He'd had an argument with his girlfri

Focus
Stories about events in the past

Functions
Expressing regret: *I'm ringing to say sorry that I didn't (go to your party).*
Making excuses: *I wanted to go but (I felt really ill).*
Asking for information: *What was wrong?; Anyway, tell me, how was (the party)?; Why was that?*
Expressing hope: *Maybe next time.*

Grammar
Past perfect: *I'd eaten too much.*

1a) Revision: adjectives

Ask learners to look at the picture. Where are the people? Now, ask them to look at the list of adjectives. Working individually, they match the names and adjectives. Get them to do this on a piece of paper, as it difficult to write on the picture.

⚠
Learners may find it difficult to label some of the people. This is deliberate, to encourage learners to use the phrases in 1b).

1a) Key
Learners' own opinions

1b)

Learners now look at the prompt box. Using this language, they exchange their opinions with a partner. When they have finished, ask the class as a whole to say how they think the people in the picture are feeling.

1c)

Tell learners they are going to hear Julia, the hostess of the party, talking to different guests. Each of the mini-dialogues gives information about some of the guests' moods. The learners' task is to write down the mood and the reason for the guest being in this particular mood.

Ask learners to read the first example, then make certain everyone knows what they are to do. Play the dialogues, stopping after each one for learners to fill in the information. If necessary, play the dialogue a second time.

CD 2/12
See the tapescripts on p. 192 of the Learner's Book.

1c) Key
1. Mike is in a bad mood because he's had an argument with his girlfriend.
2. Kim is happy because she's had some good news.
3. Vic is really angry because someone's stolen his car.
4. Jane and Paul are really proud because their daughter's just won a prize at school.
5. Sally is stressed out because her boss has given her a lot of work to do this weekend.
6. Josephine is really upset because her husband forgot her birthday.

2a)

Learners will now hear Julia, the hostess, talking to another friend, Bill, about the same party. Ask learners to look at the pictures and read the speech bubbles. Who is Julia talking about? (Mike) What about Bill? Had he been invited? (Yes, but he couldn't come to the party because he wasn't feeling well. He ate too much at lunchtime.)

First, ask learners to read the sentences on p. 90. Each of them is incorrect. Learners listen to the recording and correct the statements.

Play the recording, stopping at suitable intervals to allow learners to make changes in the statements before moving to the next.

CD 2/13
See the tapescripts on pp. 192-193 of the Learner's Book.

2a) Key
1. Bill **didn't go** to Julia's party.
2. The party was on **Friday**.
3. Mike was feeling sorry for **himself**.
4. Kim's **mother** is coming from Australia.
5. **Kim** cheered Mike up.
6. Vic was shouting and arguing **with everyone**.

2b)

Ask learners to look at the list of expressions. Elicit the meanings of any unfamiliar words or phrases. Working individually, learners complete the dialogue.

2b) Key
1. fell asleep
2. apparently
3. feeling really sorry for himself
4. showed up
5. on the way to

2c)

Play the recording again and learners check their work.

2d)

Ask learners to look at the second item in the Grammar box. Get them to establish that the Past perfect is used to refer to the earlier of two events that occurred in the past. Draw attention to the first example and point out that the form *had* is used for all six persons. In spoken English this is usually contracted to *'d* (*gone*). Learners now complete the sentences below the Grammar box.

Now, ask learners to take a coloured marker. They are to read the dialogue once again, this time underlining all the examples of the Past perfect they can find. (*I'd eaten too much at lunchtime; Apparently he'd had an argument with his girlfriend; She'd had some good news; She'd heard that her mother's coming from Australia to see her; Someone had stolen his car; He was a bit drunk – he'd been to the pub on the way to the party!*)

Select a couple of the examples and ask someone to explain the time relationships expressed in the sentences. For those examples that have no Past simple in them, what is the past event? For example, *She'd had some good news*. (She had received the news before coming to the party. Julia is relating information about this party, which is now the past event.)

Now ask learners, in pairs, to look at the sections of the dialogue that are underlined, each of which contain an example of the Past perfect. Give them a few minutes to think of some alternatives, also including the Past perfect – and then practise the dialogue their partner.

⚠

Learners may find it difficult to think of completely different sentences that fit the dialogue, so let them just modify the ones that are underlined. (See the key below.)

2d) Key

Grammar box:
had
der 3. Form
Vergangenheit

Dialogue task; some possibilities
- I think I'd had too much to drink at lunchtime …
- he'd had an argument with his boss …
- her boyfriend's coming back from the States this week.
- Someone had broken a window in his house.

3a)

Learners now refer back to 1c), where they noted down some information about the people at the party. Using this information, they enquire about the others who were there. The dialogue gave them more information about Mike, Kim and Vic. Now, they work in pairs and continue the dialogue, one taking the role of Julia, the other, the role of Bill, who wants to know more information about others at the party.

Remind them they are speaking of a past event, so the descriptions of the various people should be made using the Past perfect.

3b)

Learners now practise using the Past perfect in a very controlled exercise. Each of the sentence beginnings has an appropriate ending. Ask learners to read through the two sets and match them.

Working in pairs, one learner then reads the beginning of a sentence and the other adds the end. They then change roles, repeat the procedure with the next sentence and so on.

3b) Key
4a, 1b, 7c, 6d, 2e, 3f, 5g

4a)

Ask learners to look at the six pictures and speculate about what is happening in each one.
In pairs, they then try to decide on a logical sequence for the pictures. They can talk about the pictures using the language in the prompt box.

4a) Key
Learners' own opinions

4b)

Play the recording and learners check their answers.

CD 2/14
See the tapescript on p. 193 of the Learner's Book.

4b) Key
(Left to right)
Bottom left, upper row: 2, 6
Bottom left, lower row: 1, 3
Top right: 4, 5

4c)

4c) Key
It was a wonderful weekend because she met her husband at the bed and breakfast.

4d)

Ask learners to read through the statements, which again refer to the information in the recording. This time around, learners listen to the recording for detail, marking the correct choice as the recording moves along.

4d) Key

1. north, 2. afternoon, 3. raining, 4. foggy, 5. her car, 6. 11, 7. full, 8. a bed and breakfast place, 9. uncomfortable, 10. sunny

4e)

Learners now tell the story in their own words, taking it in turns to add more information and detail as they go along. Ask them to look at the prompt box, focusing attention on B's language. What type of language is being practised here? (turn-taking) The openers, *That's right*, and *Yes*, are used to confirm the previous speaker's comments and signal that the other speaker will take over and add something.

5a)

In this activity learners think of a memorable weekend they have had themselves. First, they should make some notes about the weekend. When was it? Where did the events happen? Who was there? What happened? They can use a dictionary or ask you or other learners for assistance.

5b)

At this point, you have two options. If the class is large and you want to keep the activity within a manageable time frame, you could ask learners to work in pairs or groups of three or four and take it in turns to relate their stories. If the class is quite small and learners are interested in hearing all the stories, you could devote more time to the activity and allow each person to relate a story.

In activities of this sort there is always the danger that learners become bored if required to listen to too many stories that are, perhaps, not all that fascinating! It might be safest, therefore, to choose the small group solution for this activity.

Technology

Unit summary

This unit focuses on recent technological developments (digital cameras and mobile phones) which influence our daily lives. In the first part of the unit learners practise shopping for digital cameras and accessories. The second part deals with telephone skills in conjunction with the topic of mobile phones. The grammar sections feature the verb *may* and several new passive tenses. There is also a longer reading text on the topic of modern communication.

Part A: May I have a look at it?

Focus
Shopping for a digital camera
Technical terminology
Buying an MP3 player

Functions
Asking for a recommendation: *Can you recommend one?*
Asking for permission: *May I have a look at ...?*
Asking for information: *What do I need to know about it?; Does it come with ...?*
Explaining something: *That refers to (the quality ...); It means you can (take about 32 pictures).*
Asking for confirmation: *So you really would recommend ...?*
Confirming: *For the price, you can't buy better.*
Expressing surprise: *What! It doesn't (come with a case)?*
Accepting a situation: *Well, I suppose I'll have to (buy one of them).*
Giving permission: *Feel free; Go ahead, it's all yours; Certainly, help yourself; Please do.*

Grammar
Modal verbs: *May I have a look at that model?*

Pronunciation
Wordstress:
2-word groups: *sound system, phone cases*, etc.

1a) Revision: adjectives and core vocabulary

Ask learners to close their books. Then, ask them to think of an airport duty free shop they have been to. What did they buy there? What did they see that was cheaper than it would have been in a regular shop? What would they not want to buy in an airport duty free shop?

Now ask learners to open their books and look at the leaflet from the Melbourne duty free shop. Ask them to use the words in the list and fill in the spaces.

1a) Key
finest Italian **handbags**
top quality leather **gloves**
lightweight **headphones**
delicious Belgian **chocolates**
chic leather **briefcases**
beautiful woollen **sweaters**

1b)

Learners listen to an announcement for the duty free shop and add the prices of the objects to the leaflet in 1a).

Does anyone happen to know how the Australian dollar compares in value to other dollar currencies or to the Euro? For the exact rate of exchange for the US$, CA$ and AU$, visit the following website, which is updated as soon as fluctuations are registered: http://www.xe.com. At the time of writing the rates were about 1 Euro = 1.28 US$; 1.68 AU$; 1.41 CA$.

CD 2/15
See the tapescript on p. 193 of the Learner's Book.

1b) Key

handbags	AU$ 35.00
gloves	AU$ 25.00
headphones	AU$ 17.39
chocolates	AU$ 9.00
briefcases	AU$ 145.00 upwards
sweaters	AU$ 49.00

2a)

Ask learners to look at the list of words, some of which will already be familiar. Rather than asking for a translation of the words, get learners to explain the meanings in English.

Now tell them they are going to hear a continuation of the previous recording, informing them of the prices of the items in the list. Before playing the recording, ask them to write all the words into the table. Then, when they hear them on the recording, they only have to note down the prices.

Follow up by eliciting the meaning of the two prepositions in this context. (*for* = *für*; *from* = *ab*). Play the recording and learners note down the preposition they hear.

CD 2/16
See the tapescript on p. 193 of the Learner's Book.

2a) Key
phone cases for $12.99
shoulder straps for $11.79
power adaptors for $3.59
DVD players from $349.00
MP3 players from $289.00
batteries from $6.69
film cards from $43.00
sound systems from $429.00

2b)

Learners now hear six (familiar) compound words and decide where the stress falls on each.

The stress is on the first part of each of them. Why do learners think this so? (The essential information is contained in the first part. For example, there are many types of systems, but this particular one is a sound system, which distinguishes it from other types of systems.)

➡ Stress on compound words (For your information only!)

Compound words are made up of two words and may be written together (*airline*) or separately (*flight attendant*).

- The stress is usually on the first word/the first part of the word: *airline, flight attendant.*
- If the first word is an adjective, there may also be a stress on the second word: *frequent flyer.*
- If the first word tells us where the second word is, there may also be a stress on the second word: *airport lounge.*

CD 2/17
See the six terms in 2b).

2b) Key
The stress is on the first word in each of the combinations.

2c)

Play the recording again. Stop after each example and ask learners to repeat.

2d)

Ask learners to look at the prompt box, which contains useful language for speculating about something. Ask them to study the phrases for 30 seconds and try to remember as many as they can. They will need the phrases when they test a partner about the prices of the various items in step 2a).

Ask learners to close their books. Write the various items from 2a) on the board, but don't add any prices. Using the items from the board, learners take it in turns to test each other on the prices.

3a)

Tell learners they will hear a dialogue in a duty free shop between a sales person and a customer who would like to buy a digital camera, but doesn't know much about them.

Ask learners to look at the list of items. Their task is to tick the items the A70 camera comes equipped with. Now ask them to close their books and simply listen to the recording and remember as much as they can. When the recording has finished, ask them to open their books and mark the items the camera comes with. Play the recording again and learners can tick any items they might have missed the first time around.

CD 2/18
See the dialogue in 3b) and the key to 3b).

3a) Key
It comes equipped with:
1. a 32MB film card
3. a one-year guarantee
5. instructions

3b)

Ask learners to look at the picture and read the speech bubble. Elicit the meaning of the verb *may*. In this context, it means *darf ich*. This is a polite way of asking for permission. *Can I*, which is also used when asking for permission, is not quite as polite.

Now ask learners to look at the questions below the picture, all of which a customer might ask when shopping for a piece of technical equipment. Working individually, learners complete the dialogue with the questions.

3b) Key
1. How much is it?
2. Have you got anything cheaper?
3. What do I need to know about it?
4. Does it come with a guarantee?
5. Can I pay in US dollars?

3c)

Play the recording again and learners check their answers.

3d)

The shopping dialogue in 3b) is rather long and passes through a number of phases before the customer actually buys the camera and pays for it. Learners should become more familiar with this dialogue before writing the new ending.

Ask learners to work in pairs and study the dialogue and identify the phases, from the opening phase (shop assistant offers help to the customer) to the closing phase (paying for the camera).

The purpose of this activity is to allow learners to familiarise themselves with the flow of the dialogue, the language, the discourse markers, etc., before making changes or additions. When learners have finished their analysis, gather the contributions, noting them in short form on the board in flowchart style.

One possible analysis:
Assistant offers help.
Customer says what he wants and asks for a recommendation.
Assistant makes two recommendations.
Customer wants more information about one of the models.
Assistant explains.
Customer asks further questions.
Assistant explains.
Customer asks for a confirmation of the recommendation.
Assistant confirms.
Assistant asks about additional accessory.
Customer expresses astonishment that it is not included.
Assistant explains why it is not included.
Customer buys camera and accessory.
Customer asks about form of payment.
Assistant completes transaction.

Learners then work in pairs and write a different ending after the line, *What! It doesn't have a case?* Ask a few pairs to read their endings to the class, then ask learners to work in pairs and practise the complete dialogue, using the endings they wrote.

Now ask learners to look at the Grammar box, which features the verb *may* in questions and *may/might* in statements. Elicit the meaning of *may* in the first two examples (asking for permission to do something). You could ask learners to read through the dialogue and find the examples of this usage in the text. (*May I look at that model?; May I see your boarding pass?)*

Ask learners to read the third example, which illustrates the use of *may/might* in statements. Tell them that *might* can also be used, and ask them to find an example in the dialogue. (*It also comes with batteries but you might want to buy rechargeable ones later.*)

Learners now read the rule and fill in the missing words.

3d) Key
Grammar box:
Erlaubnis
möglich

4a)

Ask learners to look at the pictures, then ask them to describe what they think is happening in each case. Who are the people? Where are they? What might they be asking for?

Next ask learners to look at the phrases and elicit the meanings. All of them are phrases giving permission to do something. Play the dialogues. Stop after each one so that learners can write in the expressions they hear.

CD 2/19
See the tapescript on p. 193 of the Learner's Book.

4a) Key
Picture 1: Certainly, help yourself.
Picture 2:. Go ahead. It's all yours.
Picture 3: Feel free.
Picture 4: Please do.

Ask learners to put them in order of formality, the most formal one first. (*Please do. / Certainly, help yourself. / Feel free. / Go ahead, it's all yours.*)

4b)

Using the four pictures, learners work in pairs and create new dialogues for each of the situations. They should incorporate the phrase *May I ...?*, as well as the phrases in 4a). Each of the partners should play both roles in turn.

5
Learners now work in pairs and do a roleplay on the lines of the dialogue in 3b). One learner is the shop assistant, the other a customer who wants to buy an MP3 player. The shop assistant recommends the Creative Zen Micro. The necessary information about it has been listed. This information will be useful both for the assistant and the customer. The questions that might be useful for the customer are found in the prompt box.

Before learners begin the roleplay, ask them to look through the dialogue again. This time they should use a coloured marker and underline phrases that could be useful for the roles they are about to play. The aim is not to select phrases to be used verbatim, but rather to revise the language used in this situation. When they have finished this, they do their own roleplay using the information given in Step 5.

Part B: 100 million mobile phones were sold in 1997

Focus
Formal and informal telephone language
Telephone behaviour
Advantages and disadvantages of mobile phones

Functions
Telephoning:
- Offering assistance: *How may I help you?*
- Putting someone through: *Would you hold the line, please?; Can you hang on a moment? I'll see if he's around.*
- Saying someone is not available: *I'm afraid her extension is engaged at the moment; Sorry, he's not here.*
- Offering to take a message: *Would you like to/Do you want to leave a message?*
- Saying you'll call back: *I'll call again this afternoon; I'll ring later on.*

Saying goodbye (informally): *Cheers.*
Agreeing: *I completely agree with the point that ...*
Disagreeing: *I'm not sure I agree with the idea that ...; I don't agree at all with the writer when she says .... I think ...*

Grammar
Passive forms:
- Present simple: *Mobile phones are now used ...*
- Past simple: *100 million phones were sold.*
- Present perfect: *The mobile phone business has been developed ...*
- Past perfect: *You knew it had been delivered ...*
- Modal verbs/auxiliaries: *Mobile phones can be used ...; Microphones will be implanted ...*

1a) Revision: the verb *may*

Ask learners to read the questions in the left-hand column, then read the situations in which one might use them.

Working individually, learners match them up by drawing lines from the question to an appropriate situation. There may be more than one possibility for several of the questions.

1a) Key
Some possibilities:

on the phone
May I leave a message?

in a restaurant
May I have the bill, please?
May I pay with a credit card?
May I speak to the manager?

in a shop
May I try them on?
May I have a look?

at a dinner party
May I have some more?

on a bus or train
May I sit here?

1b)

Learners now work individually and complete the four mini-dialogues with expressions from 1a). They then practise the mini dialogues in pairs. Remind them to change roles.

1b) Key
1. May I have some more?
2. May I try them on?
3. May I have the bill please?; May I pay with a credit card?
4. May I speak to the manager?; May I leave a message

1c)

Ask learners to look at 1b) again and write the first line of Dialogue 1 on a piece of paper. Working in pairs they use that line as the start of a new mini-dialogue of their own. It should include a question with *May ...?* They repeat the process with the first lines of Dialogues, 2, 3 and 4.

2a)

In this activity learners unjumble two telephone calls, an informal one to a friend and a more formal one to a company. The telephoning phrases are jumbled, but if learners pay attention to whether the person being called is male or female, they will have little difficulty sorting out the phrases and putting them into the correct dialogue. As an additional help, several phrases have already been written into the dialogue.

Ask learners to read through the phrases, then read them aloud yourself, taking care to use appropriate intonation. Ask learners to repeat after you. Don't comment on the language register at this point, however. Learners will work with this aspect of the language in 2c).

➡ Cheers
This expression is used in three different ways:
1. before you begin to drink an alcoholic drink;
2. (in the UK) as an informal alternative to 'Thanks';
3. (in the UK) as an informal alternative to 'Goodbye'.

2a) Key
10, 2, 1, 7, 8, 3, 9, 4, 12, 6, 11, 5
(Call 1: 1–6; Call 2: 7–12)

English at home

Unit summary

This unit focuses on using English in one's own surroundings, in particular on helping English-speaking tourists find their way around and suggesting things that might make their visit more memorable and enjoyable. The grammar features are the verbs *shall* (for making suggestions), *should and ought to*, and reported speech.

Part A: You really ought to go to the Albertina

Focus
Using English in one's own surroundings
Helping English-speaking visitors
Suggestions for tourists

Functions
Making suggestions/recommendations: *Shall we (stop and have lunch)?*; We should ask the waiter; *You really ought to go to ...*; *You shouldn't forget to visit (the cathedral).*
Agreeing: *Anywhere is fine with me.*
Expressing relief: *I thought you'd never ask.*
Estimating: *It shouldn't (take you more than 20 minutes).*
Interrupting someone: *Excuse me for intruding but ...*

Grammar
Modal verbs:
Shall we stop and have lunch here?
You really ought to go to the Albertina.
We should ask the waiter.
You shouldn't forget the Vienna Art Museum.

What you need
Unit 10A, 4a): Have a dictionary or two available for this step.

1a) Revision: adverbs of frequency

In this activity learners revise the adverbs of frequency by identifying the ways they use English in their own surroundings. In sentences 1 – 5 they select an appropriate adverb from the choices given. Then, in 6 – 8, they answer questions about the use of English in their own country.

1a) Key
Learners' own answers

1b)

Ask learners to look at the prompt box, then work in groups of three and discuss their answers from 1a). Ask each group to give feedback on one of the points discussed in their group.

2a)

Ask learners to look at the picture at the top of the page. Can anyone say which city it is? Has anyone been to Vienna? Do they recognise the building? (the Albertina). What is it and what can you see there? Now get learners to look at the picture at the bottom of the page. What are the people doing? What does the question in the bubble mean?

Next ask learners to read the jumbled dialogue and number the segments in the correct sequence. To make things easier, the individual parts have been grouped together. Point out that they needn't worry about the underlined words at the moment. These will be used later in step 2c). Remind learners to use pencil when doing the task, as they may want to make changes before they have finished.

➡ The Albertina
The Albertina was founded in 1738 and is one of Europe's foremost museums. Its collection of drawings is one the largest in the world and it houses, among other treasures, a large collection of Dürer drawings. For more information about its history, collections and exhibitions, see:
http://www.albertina.at

2a) Key
7, 3, 1, 5, 8, 4, 6, 2

2b)

Play the recording and learners check their answers.

CD 2/22
▲ What an amazing place. Vienna really is a beautiful city.
○ Yes, yes. It's lovely but ...
▲ But what? Aren't you enjoying yourself?
○ Yes, I am, but we've been walking all morning. I'm hungry and I need to put my feet up for half an hour.
▲ Shall we stop and have lunch instead?
○ That's a great idea. I thought you'd never ask.
▲ That looks like a nice place. Shall we eat there?
○ Anywhere is fine with me.

2c)

Before learners practise the dialogue, ask them to take a piece of paper and write it out in full in the correct order so that, when they practise the dialogue, they will be focusing on the language rather than on the problem of getting the order right. Learners then work in pairs and practise the dialogue. Remind them to change roles.

Learners now look at the jumbled dialogues and underline the words in their hand-written text that are underlined in the jumbled dialogue. Working together, they decide what changes they would like to make, then practise the new dialogue together. Ask one or two pairs to read their new version.

Finally ask learners to look at the Grammar box. How is the verb *shall* used in these examples? (to make a suggestion). Learners read the rule and fill in the missing word.

2c) Key
Grammar box:
Vorschlag

2d)

Ask learners to look at the six pictures and read the questions under them. Working individually, they make a suggestion for each of the situations. They could then compare their ideas in pairs or small groups and decide which they like best.

2d) Key
Some possibilities:
1st pic.: No idea. Shall we take a taxi?
2nd pic.: I don't know. Shall we ask someone for help?
3rd pic.: Shall we sit down and rest?
4th pic.: Shall we have lunch first?
5th pic.: Shall we take my camera?
6th pic.: Shall we go in?

3a)

Tell learners they are now going to hear a continuation of the dialogue in 2b). Ask them to read the questions, then close their books and just listen to the dialogue. After that, they open their books again and answer any of the questions they can.

Play the dialogue and again and learners answer any questions that they couldn't the first time round.

➡ Kunsthistorisches Museum, Vienna
This museum was opened in 1891 and houses one of the most important collections in the world. For lots of interesting information visit the khm website: http://www.khm.at

CD 2/23
See the dialogue in 3b).

3a) Key
1. the Kunsthistorische
2. the woman
3. not more than 20 minutes walking
4. a Chagall exhibition
5. Vienna Art Museum

3b)

Ask learners to read through the dialogue. Then, ask them to look at the sentence in the bubble and elicit the meaning.

Learners now focus their attention on the Grammar box. Both *ought to* and *should* mean much the same as *sollen*. What differentiates them from each other in form? (*Ought* takes *to* + the infinitive, whereas *should* requires only the infinitive.)

Now ask learners to read through the dialogue again. Working in groups of three, they think of an ending to the dialogue and write it in their books. Circulate and help with the grammar as necessary.

Learners then practise the dialogue with their new text. Remind them to change roles so that everyone has the opportunity to practise their new text.

3b) Key
Learners' own ideas

Grammar box:
Vorschläge (und) Empfehlungen

4a)

In this activity learners personalise vocabulary by making lists of things they would recommend a tourist to do: one list is for interesting things in their own town or city; the other for things they would recommend to someone visiting their country.

The lists can include everything from food and drink to exhibitions, sports events, music festivals, sights ... in short, anything they think might be of real interest to the tourist.

4a) Key
Learners' own suggestions

4b)

Before learners commence with the pair work, ask them to look at the prompt box, which features different ways of making suggestions.

Learners now work in pairs and take it in turn to be the tourist. The local person makes recommendations using items from their own lists.

Part B: He said it opened at nine

Focus
Museum visits
Passing on a telephone message
Marc Chagall
Describing works of art

Functions
Apologising: *Oh, sorry. My mistake,*
Expressing enthusiasm: *Great! I can hardly wait to (see the paintings).*
Expressing surprise: *But hold on …*
Expressing disbelief: *I mean, come on!*
Making a suggestion: *I think we'd better (have a guide), don't you?*

Grammar
Reported speech: *He said it opened at nine; She said she'd read a book about him; He told us we could take photos; He said there would be a guided tour.*

What you need
Unit 10B, 2d): One photocopy of p. 116 for each group of three learners.

1a) Revision: making suggestions using *shall*

In this activity learners match the numbers of the pictures with one of the suggestions from the list. First, ask them to cover the right-hand column of the page with a piece of paper. Then, ask them to look at the pictures depicting common tourist situations. Call on various learners to describe the situations in the pictures.

Ask learners to uncover the right-hand column and read the suggestions. Learners then work individually and match the pictures with the situations.

1a) Key
5a, 6b, 1c, 3d, 2e, 4f

1b)

Learners now read six statements about the importance of art and the arts in everyday life. They then tick the statements they personally agree with.

When they have finished, carry on to the next step.

1b) Key
Learners' own answers

1c)

Learners now work in groups of three and compare their responses to the statements in 1b).

First, ask them to look at the prompt box, then express their own preferences and comment on their partners'. They shouldn't worry if it is difficult to make a suitable suggestion in response. The important thing is for them to exchange their views.

2a)

Learners now hear two people talking about a Chagall exhibition.

Ask them to read the five sentences first of all. They should just listen to the recording the first time around. Play the recording without a pause. Learners can now make corrections they are certain about. Then, play the recording again, using the pause button if necessary, to allow learners to correct the other statements as the recording progresses.

CD 2/24
See the dialogue in 2b).

2a) Key
1. Albertina art gallery
2. Picasso
3. 10 am
4. It costs 12 euros.
5. No flash photography allowed

2b)

Learners look at the phrases below the picture on p. 112 and use them to complete the dialogue.

2b) Key
1. much else
2. My mistake.
3. hardly wait
4. come on
5. I guess not
6. we'd better

2c)

Play the recording and learners check their work.

2d)

Ask learners to look at the Grammar box. Focus their attention on the first two examples. Point out the differences between direct and indirect speech, e.g. the use of the verb *said* and tense shift from Present simple tense (direct speech) to Past simple tense (reported speech). Proceed in the same manner with the remaining examples.

What do they notice about punctuation of the examples in the box? (Unlike German there is no comma separating the main clause from the relative clause in reported speech.)

What is the difference between *say* and *tell*? (There is no personal direct object after *say*. There is always a personal direct object or someone's name after *tell.*)

Now ask learners to look at the picture at the top of the page on the left and read the bubble, which highlights one example of reported speech in the dialogue. Learners now go through the dialogue again and mark any examples of indirect speech they can find:

But you told me you'd read a book about him.
But the waiter said it opened at nine.
I'm sure the waiter said it was free.
I don't think he told us that.
He told us we could take photos.
Did he say there would be a guided tour?

Finally, learners read the rule below the Grammar box and complete it, then practise the dialogue again in pairs.

Extra activity
For more practice of reported speech, make one photocopy of p. 116 for each group of three learners and cut up the cards. One of the group shuffles and deals out each set of cards (Caller and Message) separately.

Set the situation by telling your learners that their answering machines are not working, so everybody had to take messages for everyone else. They don't know who took their messages, so they have to ask the others and find out what the caller wanted.

Each player looks at the their Caller cards and takes it in turn to guess who might have the matching Message card, e.g. *Have you got a message from my boss?*

The player who has the Message card passes on the message, e.g. *Yes, I have. He said you could go home early this afternoon.* The Message card is then handed over to the person who asked.

If the person asked does not have the relevant message, the 'asker' has to wait until his/her turn comes round again. The game continues until all the cards have been matched.

2d) Key
Grammar box:
Present simple wird zu **Past simple**, Past simple wird zu **Past Perfect**, *can* wird zu **could**, *will* zu **would.**
Entsprechend wird z.B. das Present progressive zum **Past Progressive**, Present Perfect zum **Past Perfect.**

3a)
In this step learners listen to a woman leaving a telephone call for her parents. Ask them to first read the incomplete statements. Then, play the recording and learners fill in the missing information.

CD 2/25
See the tapescript on p. 194 of the Learner's Book.

3a) Key
1. Vienna, 2. awful, 3. food, 4. good, 5. Kunsthistorische, 6. waiter, 7. talk, 8. Monday

3b)
Before learners pass on the information in the message, ask them to work individually and transform each of the direct statements into reported speech.

Check before carrying on to the pair activity.

Now ask learners to turn their written versions over. Working in pairs, they take it in turns to pass on the details of the message using reported speech.

3b) Key
1. She said they were in Vienna.
2. She said the weather was awful.
3. She said James didn't like the food very much.
4. She said they were having a good time.
5. She said they had visited the Kunsthistorische Museum.
6. She said a waiter had helped them find it.
7. She said she couldn't talk for very long.
8. She said she'd phone again on Monday.

4a)
The following series of steps focuses on the artist Marc Chagall. Many learners will know his work or at least recognise it when they see it.

Start with a brainstorm to find out what the class already knows about Chagall. You could organise the information they come up with on the board in the form of a word map, using categories such as *biography, works, exhibitions/museums*.

Now tell learners they are going to hear a museum guide talking about Chagall. Ask them to look at the dates. They will have to listen quite carefully: the dates are not all given in a chronological sequence and 1952, for instance, when Chagall married a second time, is not actually spoken (the guide says '*Eight years later …*').

Play the recording, using the pause button at intervals to allow learners enough time to fill in the missing information.

CD 2/26
See the tapescript on p. 194 of the Learner's Book.

4a) Key
1887 Chagall was born.
1915 He married his first wife Bella.
1923 He went to live in France.

1937 He became a French citizen.
1944 Bella died.
1952 He married a second time.
1973 The Chagall Museum opened.
1985 He designed windows for Reims Cathedral shortly before he died.

4b)

In this listening activity learners listen to the same recording for more detail. First, ask them to read the questions. See how much of the information they managed to retain before you play the recording.

4b) Key

1. 97
2. Paris and Provence (near Vence)
3. in the USA
4. designed opera sets and stained glass windows for churches
5. Nice

5a)

Here learners look at three celebrated paintings and talk about their own preferences in art.

Ask learners to look at the list of words and elicit the meanings of each. Then, ask them to look at the paintings and decide which of the words describe them best.

A: Marc Chagall. *Daphnis and Chloe*
This is a post-impressionist lithographic print.

B: David Hockney. *Mr and Mrs Clark and Percy*
This is a 'pop art' portrait., in acrylic paints on canvas.

C: Jan van Eyck. *Arnolfini's Wedding* (also known *as The Arnolfini Marriage)*
This is a fifteenth-century Flemish portrait, painted in oils on wood.

➡ Daphnis and Chloe

The story of Daphnis and Chloe is attributed to the Greek poet Longus (second century A.D.) and has served through the ages as the inspiration for many love stories, including *Romeo and Juliet.* The classical romance tells of the adventures of two foundling children raised by adoptive parents who are shepherds on the Aegean island of Lesbos. Both children are found with rich tokens, suggesting they might be of noble birth. As the children grow older, they discover that their friendship has developed into love, but they are uncertain as to how they should proceed. Before realizing their true fate, they experience many difficulties, but are always protected by the god Pan.

➡ David Hockney (1937 -)

Hockney is a British painter, draughtsman, printmaker, photographer and designer. He had attained international success by the time he was in his mid-twenties and has since consolidated his position as the best-known British artist of his generation. His success is not only based on his work but also on his colourful personality. A film about him, *A Bigger Splash*, (1974) enjoyed considerable popularity. *Mr and Mrs Clark and Percy* (1970) hangs in the Tate Gallery in London and is one of Hockney's best-known and most popular works.

➡ Jan van Eyck (died 1441)

The '*Arnolfini Wedding*' portrait of 1434 is undoubtedly one of the greatest masterpieces of Northern Renaissance painting and one that has engaged the interest of art historians over the centuries. The title has traditionally been given to the painting because it was thought to be a form of 'wedding certificate' for Giovanni Arnolfini and Giovanna Cenami, who married in Brügge/Bruges in 1434.

The picture, which can be seen in London's National Gallery, is loaded with symbolism. Almost every object portrayed conveys the event's sanctity, specifically the holiness of matrimony:

- the clogs – indicate the event is taking place on holy ground;
- the dog – symbolizes fidelity;
- the bedpost's crowning ornament, a tiny statue of Saint Margaret – patron saint of childbirth;
- the oranges on the chest – fertility;
- the single candle burning; the mirror – all-seeing eye of God;
- the medallions in the frame of the mirror – scenes from the Passion of Christ.

Many have thought that Giovanna Cenami is depicted as pregnant. However, most experts agree that this is not the case. She is simply holding up her gown in a manner that was very typical for the period.

5b)

Ask learners to look at the prompt box. Elicit the meaning of any unfamiliar words. Learners then work in groups of three and describe each of the paintings. They should describe them in as much detail as possible. This could include descriptions of the figures, description of detail in the background/foreground, the relationship of the figures to each other, etc.

Ask learners speculate on the date of the works.

- Daphnis and Chloe: this one of a suite of prints on the legend, published in 1961
- Mr and Mrs Clark and Percy: 1970
- Arnolfini's Wedding: 1434

5c)

Learners now personalise the topic by talking to each other about the kinds of painting they like best and the kinds they don't like at all. If the group is interested in art and art history, this discussion could be quite intensive and detailed. If, however, you find that the majority of learners are not particularly interested in art then the activity is best kept short!

People like us

Unit summary

The first part of the unit focuses on travel situations and travellers, in particular on complaining and the negative aspects of travel and service. The second part of the unit focuses on probability, star signs (the signs of the Zodiac) and horoscopes. The grammar sections feature relative clauses with verbs + prepositions as well as the verbs *make/let* + infinitive without *to*.

Part A: The room you've put me in is too small

Focus
Complaints in hotels and other public places
Typical travellers
Character attributes

Functions
Complaining: *I'm not very happy with …*
Expressing regret: *I'm sorry to hear that; That's a shame, sir; I'm sorry you think that, sir.*
Asking for details: *What exactly is the problem?*
Playing for time: *Let me see.*
Responding to a complaint: *I'm afraid I can't really help you. The man you need to talk to is …*
Expressing dissatisfaction: *Well, that's no good; That's exactly what I'm afraid of; You really don't seem very interested in helping me at all.*
Countering: *Well, I do.*

Grammar
Relative clauses with verbs + prepositions: *The room (that) you've put me in is too small.*

What you need
Unit 11A, 3c/3d): A few dictionaries if learners don't usually bring their own.
Unit 11A, 3g): One photocopy of p. 117 for each group of three or four learners.

1a) Revision: reported speech

In this activity learners revise reported speech by focusing their attention on complaints, the topic that follows. Ask learners to look at the five statements and the places one might hear them. Then, working individually, they match each complaint with one of the places.

1a) Key
5 – at a theatre box office
4 – in an estate agent's
3 – at the doctor's
1 – at the ticket office of a company that runs sightseeing tours
2 – in a chemist's

1b)

Learners now change the reported statements in 1a) into direct speech.

Before they begin the activity, you might like to revise the rules of reported speech. Elicit the rules using the first example in 1a) and 1b). (*Lunch is included. – You told us that lunch was included.*) If necessary, remind learners that they can consult the grammar section at the back of the book, p.169, which has good overview of the structures.

1b) Key
1. Lunch is included.
2. You don't need a prescription for this medication.
3. If you take this medicine, you'll feel better.
4. The house is close to the shops.
5. The view from the circle is good.

1c)

Working individually, learners now write complaints that might be heard at one of the places on the list. They are to formulate the complaints using reported speech, directing the complaint to an unnamed individual, e.g. *You said / told me ….*

1c) Key
Some possibilities:

In a restaurant
You told us the vegetables were fresh.
You said the red wine was light.

On a railway station platform
You said the train left from track 10.
You told me the train would be on time.

At the reception in a hotel lobby
You said there was a hairdryer in the room.
You told me my room was quiet.

2a)

Ask learners to work in pairs and make a list of things that could go wrong in hotel situations.

2a) Key
Learners' own ideas

2b)

In this activity learners consider how they would react in the various situations. Before they start, ask learners to look at the prompt box at the top of p. 117, which features *if* clauses. Ask learners to look at the verb forms. Which tenses are used? What is the speaker expressing by using these tenses? (improbability) If learners feel uncertain about the structure, ask them to refer to p.169 for more information.

Begin the activity by making a complaint yourself, e.g. *The room is too noisy*, then asking another learner to make a suggestion.

Now, ask learners to stand up and walk around for this activity. They talk to each other, one person stating a complaint, the other suggesting something one might do in such a situation. After each has had an opportunity to make a complaint, they move on to someone else with a different complaint. Allow the activity to run until each person has spoken to four or five different people.

2c)

Learners now hear a conversation between a hotel guest and a person at the reception. The guest, Mr. Swan, is dissatisfied with several things.

Ask learners to look at the six items on the list. Play the recording and learners mark the items Mr Swan mentions.

CD 2/27
See the dialogue in 2d).

2c) Key
1. the size of his room
3. the restaurant
5. the 'receptionist'

2d)

Ask learners to look at the list of adjectives describing people's character. Elicit the meanings from the learners. Mention both meanings of *funny*, i.e. *humorous* or *strange*, *odd*, as this word is often a source of confusion for learners.

Ask learners to read the dialogue and decide which adjectives fit Mr Swan and the hotel manager. Play the recording again. The nuances of speech may play a role in their decisions.

2e)

Ask learners to look at the prompt box. Elicit the meaning of the statements. Make certain that they are aware of the meanings of *quite* and *definitely*.

In pairs, learners then compare their ideas about the two people.

2f)

Learners now practise the dialogue in pairs, with emotion!

When they have finished, you might like to focus on what happens when the stress is shifted around a sentence. Take a sentence like: *You don't seem very interested in helping me at all* and read it several times, stressing different words each time *(You; don't; seem; helping; me; at all).* Ask learners to decide how the sense changes in each case.

Some other segments that learners could play with:

- *I'm not very happy with the service that I've been getting at your hotel.*
- *That's exactly what I'm afraid of.*
- *I am the manager , sir. Now, how can I help you?*

2g)

Look back at the dialogue one more time. Is the customer likely get satisfaction? If not, why not? Point out that in English-speaking cultures it is usually better to express yourself politely and diplomatically even when you feel you have good grounds for complaining. Get learners to look at the customer's utterances and decide how they could be made more courteous. When everyone has finished, ask the pairs to act out their new versions.

Now ask learners to look at the Grammar box. In informal speaking and writing, the preposition is put at the end of the clause and the relative pronoun is often left out. Learners read the rules and fill in the missing information.

⚠
The preposition can also be put at the beginning of the clause *(e.g. The room* ***in which*** *you have put me …).* However this construction is normally only used in very formal written English and is probably dying out, so there is no need to mention it to your learners.

Extra Activity: Memory
To give learners more of a feel for relative clauses where the relative pronoun is dropped, divide the class into groups of three or four. Make one copy of p. 117 for each group and cut up the cards.

Learners shuffle the cards and spread them face down on a table. One learner picks up any two cards. If they fit together to make a sentence, the learner keeps the cards. If not, they are replaced face down on the table and the next player has a turn. The game finishes when all the cards have been matched. The person with the most cards wins.

2g) Key
Customer (some possibilities):

I'm not very happy with the service that I've been getting at your hotel.
→ I'm a bit unhappy about the service here.

Well, for a start, the room that you've put me in is too small.
→ I find the room a bit small.

I had dinner in your restaurant yesterday, and my meal was awful, if I'm being honest.
→ I had dinner in the restaurant yesterday and didn't enjoy the meal very much.

Well, that's no good. I'm leaving tomorrow.
→ Unfortunately, that's too late. I'm leaving tomorrow.

That's exactly what I'm afraid of.
→ Yes, please do.

You don't really seem very interested in helping me at all.
→ You don't seem too concerned about my complaints.

I'd like to speak to the manager.
→ Could I please speak to the manager?

Extra activity:
The hotel we're + staying in is very expensive.
The guided tour + we took in London was not very interesting.
The most exciting + thing I've ever tried is bungee jumping.
That MP3 player she + bought at the duty free shop doesn't work
The pictures we looked + at in the museum were all very modern.
The cruise + he took last year went to the Caribbean.
The person you + should talk to is the director.
New York is a city that + never sleeps.
That's the man + who helped us out yesterday.
The opera + I went to last night was excellent.

Grammar box:
zusammenstehen
hinter

3a)

These texts deal with three types of traveller: the worrier, the backpacker, and the travel bore. Write the three types on the board and brainstorm their characteristics. How would learners expect them to behave?

Learners now skim the texts (ignoring the gaps in brackets for the moment) and match each with one of the three traveller types. Set a time limit of two or three minutes so that there will be a sense of urgency to get through the text.

3a) Key
A: The travel bore
B: The backpacker
C: The worrier

3b)

Ask learners to read the five sentences, which have been removed from the texts in 3a). Where would they fit best?

3b) Key
1b, 2e, 3c, 4a, 5d

3c)

First, ask learners to read through the definitions and make certain they understand them. Then, working individually, learners match each of them with one of the traveller types, according to their own perception of these travellers.

Learners should be prepared to say why they made their choices, e.g. *Rucksack travellers are often inconsiderate, because they block the aisles with their rucksacks*. Call on various learners for their opinions, asking them to give reasons for their choices.

⚠
Some of the characteristics could apply to more than one of the traveller types. The important thing is that learners give their reasons for putting people into a particular category.

3c) Key
Some possibilities:
The travel bore: boring, inconsiderate, talkative
The backpacker: enthusiastic, idealistic, inconsiderate, talkative, tight-fisted
The worrier: anxious, impatient, impolite

3d)

Learners now match the adjectives in 3c) with their opposites. Note the possibility of using a prefix to construct the opposite, e.g. *polite/impolite; considerate/inconsiderate*.

➡ Prefixes + adjectives

il-	before *-l*	*(illegal, illiterate)*
im-	before *-m, -p*	*(immature, impolite)*
ir-	before *-r*	*(irrelevant, irreversible)*

Apart from these examples there is no helpful guide as to which prefixes can be used where. Some words can take more than one prefix, changing their meaning as they do (e.g. *disinterested/uninterested* and *disorganised/unorganised*). Such words simply have to be learnt.

3d) Key
See the tapescript for 3e).

Also possible:
polite – rude
interesting – uninteresting

3e)

Play the recording and learners check their work. Note that the recording includes *unrealistic*, although this does not occur in 3c).

CD 2/28
polite – impolite
considerate – inconsiderate
patient – impatient
realistic – idealistic (or unrealistic)
interesting – boring
enthusiastic – uninterested
calm – anxious
generous – tight-fisted
quiet – talkative

3f)

Learners listen to the recording again and mark the stress on the words as they hear them. Play the recording again, stopping after each word for learners to repeat in chorus.

The male speaker stresses the 'negative' prefixes in the right-hand column. These words could also be stressed as follows: impolite, inconsiderate, impatient, unrealistic, uninterested.

3f) Key
polite – impolite
considerate - inconsiderate
patient – impatient
realistic – idealistic or unrealistic
interesting – boring
enthusiastic – uninterested
calm – anxious
generous – tight-fisted
quiet – talkative

4

Learners now personalise the language they have used in this unit so far by thinking about types of travellers they have come across and describing them to a partner.

First, give learners time to work individually. They should think of a traveller they have met or observed, then make notes about the characteristics of this person. Their description should include personal characteristics as well as a short anecdote which throws more light on their character.

When they have finished, ask them to walk around and tell each other about their person. Gather feedback by asking one or two learners to describe an interesting person/type they heard about from someone else.

Part B: Let someone else look after you

Focus
Expressing probability
Star signs (Signs of the Zodiac)
Horoscopes
Personal characteristics

Functions
Asking about probability: *Do you think you'll (go out for a meal this weekend)?; What's the chance of (you going out for a meal this weekend)?; How likely (are you to go out for a meal this weekend)?*
Expressing probability: *I might; There's a small chance I might; It's difficult to say because ...*

Grammar
Verbs
make/let + object + verb in the infinitive without *to: A TV programme will **make** you **think** about your health; Don't **let** people **push** you around.*

1a) Revision: expressing probability

Ask learners to look at the probability scale. Get them to underline *definitely will* and then identify other words on the scale that express probability (*a good chance, a 50/50 chance, small chance, definitely won't).*

Next, ask learners to read the list of things that might happen and mark each one according to the probability of its happening to them over the next week.

When learners have finished, ask them to comment on one thing from the list by saying how probable it is that this will occur, e.g. *I'll definitely go out for a meal.*

1a) Key
Learners' own answers

1b)

Tell learners they will now hear two people talking about the three things listed in the table and the likelihood of their happening. Learners mark the degree of probability according to what they hear. Nigel, for example, thinks there a small chance that he might have an accident, as he is going skiing.

CD 2/29
See the tapescript on p. 194 of the Learners's Book.

1b) Key

	Nigel	Helen
having an accident	1	1
spending a lot of money	4	0
going out for a meal	4	3

1c)

Ask learners to look at the three prompt boxes. These present three ways of saying the same thing, from simple to complicated. Ask learners to read them carefully, as they are all very useful. One should note both question and response, which function as a pair.

Learners now work in pairs and talk about the various events in 1a). They should take it in turns to ask each other about the likelihood of these things happening. Remind them to practise all three models.

2a)

In this activity learners match the signs of the Zodiac and the times of year they are associated with. Learners may or may not be familiar with these signs. If they aren't, they should just guess.

2a) Key

March 21 – April 19:	Aries
April 20 – May 20:	Taurus
May 21 – June 20:	Gemini
June 21 – July 20:	Cancer
July 21 – August 22:	Leo
August 23 – Sept. 22:	Virgo
September 23 – Oct. 22:	Libra
October 23 – Nov. 21:	Scorpio
November 22 – Dec. 21:	Sagittarius
December 22 – Jan. 19:	Capricorn
January 20 – Feb. 18:	Aquarius
February 19 – March 20:	Pisces

2b)

Play the recording and learners check their answers.

CD 2/30
See the key to 2a).

➡ Star signs (Signs of the Zodiac)
The 'English' names for the signs of the Zodiac are all Latin:
Aries: the ram; Taurus: the bull; Gemini: the twins; Cancer: the crab; Leo: the lion; Virgo: the virgin; Libra: the balance or the scales; Scorpio: the scorpion; Sagittarius: the archer; Capricorn: the horned goat; Aquarius: the water-carrier; Pisces: the fishes.

Western astrology derives from the work of Babylonian astronomers who divided the eliptic into twelve equal zones of celestial longitude at some point in the first millennium B.C. Chinese astrology associates months and years with a cycle of twelve animals that influence human destinies for the good or bad.

2c)

Learners practice pronouncing the signs of the Zodiac. Call them out and ask learners to repeat in chorus.

2d)

Give learners a few minutes to think of people they get on well with and whose star sign they know. They should consider why they get on well with these people. Do they, for example, share some of the same character traits?

Learners then tell a partner about the people they chose, mentioning their star sign.

2e)

Learners now walk around and find other people who share the same signs as the people they described to their partner.

3a)

Ask learners to read the horoscope quickly for gist. They should ignore the gaps in brackets for the moment; their only task is to decide whether the week will be a good or bad one for Libras.

3a) Key

This will be a bad week for Libras.

3b)

Learners now work individually and write the days of the week under the picture depicting the events described in the horoscope.

3b) Key

Bottom left-hand column:
left: Wednesday; right: Friday

Top right-hand column, first row:
left: Monday; right: Thursday

Top right-hand column, second row:
left: weekend; right: Tuesday

3c)

Ask learners to read the definitions, then match them with the expressions in italics in 3a).

When they have finished, ask learners to look at the Grammar box, which features the verbs *make* and *let* + the infinitive without *to*. Get them to read the examples and fill in the missing word below.

3c) Key

Horoscope:
unexpected delivery: 5
push you around: 1
chance meeting: 3
get through: 6
catch up on lots of news: 2
keep your mind off: 4

Grammar box:
to

3d)

Learners now choose one of the four famous people in the pictures. The symbols of their star signs are printed next to their names (Camilla Parker-Bowles: Cancer; Hillary Clinton: Scorpio; Bill Gates: Scorpio; Bono: Taurus).

Working in pairs, learners write a horoscope for the coming week for the person they chose. It can be either positive, negative or a mixture of both. It should be structured along the lines of the horoscope in 3a), although it need not be so lengthy.

Give learners about ten minutes to write their texts. When everyone has finished, ask various pairs to read their texts to the class. Note any important grammar errors and deal with them later.

3d) Key

Learners' own texts

4a)

Learners will hear a recording of two people talking about two of the signs of the Zodiac and describing the characteristics of people born under these signs.

Ask learners to read through the statements. Tell them that they should just listen to the recording the first time around.

Play the recording again, stopping often for learners to consider what they have heard. The statements about Sagittarians are clear-cut, but they will have to listen carefully to the description of the Capricorns.

⚠
Note that this not a straightforward True/False task. Learners are asked to tick only those sentences which are **definitely** true.

CD 2/31

See the tapescript on pp. 194 – 195 of the Learner's Book.

4a) Key

The following statements are definitely true:
1, 3, 5, 7, 8.

4b)

Learners choose four adjectives for each of the star signs discussed in 4a).

Play the recording once more, pausing at intervals to allow learners to select appropriate adjectives and write them into the list.

4b) Key

Some possibilities:
Capricorns are organised, patient, considerate, serious.
Sagittarians are impatient, easy-going, enthusiastic, funny.

4c)

Learners now talk about their opinions regarding horoscopes and other methods of 'fortune-telling'.

Give learners plenty of time to read the questions and discuss them. Keep an eye on things and when you have the feeling that interest is flagging, stop the group work and carry on to the next step.

4d)

Learners write a short description of themselves or of someone they know quite well on a piece of paper, using as much of the new vocabulary as possible.

Allow learners about ten minutes to complete the writing task, then collect the descriptions.

4e)

Read out one of the descriptions to the class. Learners guess the person's star sign.

(This really is simply a guessing game, as the only information supplied in the unit is about Capricorns and Sagittarians. However many learners will know something about the other signs and be able to inform those who do not.)

⚠

The information gap activity is not concerned with Unit 11. This information goes with the activity in Unit 4, Part B, p. 47.

India

Unit summary

The unit focuses on India and visiting India as a tourist. In the first part of the unit learners find out some interesting facts about India and talk about what they should consider when travelling there. The second part of the unit centres on storytelling. Learners write a short story themselves using elements from a traditional Indian story. The grammar features are the infinitive of purpose, the *for + -ing* structure, and questions in reported speech.

Part A: I need something to …

Focus
Facts about India
Travelling to India
Advice for tourists

Functions
Explaining what you need: *I need one of those things to …; Have you got one of those things for …*

Grammar
Infinitive of purpose: *I need one of those things* ***to put*** *this plug into the wall.*
for + -ing: *Have you got one of those things* ***for taking*** *a temperature?*

What you need
Unit 12A, 3d): Learners will need their dictionaries in this step.

1a) Revision: core vocabulary

Before starting work on this unit, ask whether anyone in your class has been to India. If so, they might like to say something about their trip.

If no one has been there, you could begin by asking learners what words they associate with India and gather these on the board. You might also want to take a map of India and locate the cities that are mentioned in the unit, e.g. New Delhi, Mumbai, Calcutta, Agra, Goa, as well as any other places learners might mention.

Now, ask learners to look at the picture of the Taj Mahal. In the upper half of the picture there are five sentences from an advert for India. Working individually, learners complete the sentences, selecting the correct option from the list of words in the lower half of the picture.

1a) Key
1. make, 2. you well, 3. our, 4. ought, 5. let

➡ Taj Mahal
The Taj Mahal, which is pictured here, is on the banks of the Yamuna River in the city of Agra, in the northern Indian state of Uttar Pradesh. It was built in memory of Arjumand Bano Begum, who won the heart of a Mogul prince. She was married at the age of 21 to Emperor Jahangir's third son Prince Khurram and remained loyally at his side until her untimely death.

In AD 1628 Khurram became king after a bloody battle of succession; from then on he took the name Shahjahan or 'King of the World' and showered his beloved Begum with many titles; she became Mumtaz Mahal, the Exalted of the Palace, and Mumtaz-ul-Zamani, the Exalted of the Age. In 1631, Shahjahan went on an expedition to the south and his beloved wife accompanied him, as she always did. But, unfortunately, she died in childbirth at Burhanpur. Shahjahan was inconsolable and contemporary chronicles tell of the royal court mourning for two years. There was no music, no feasting and no celebration of any kind.

1b)

In this activity, learners can test their own knowledge of India. Ask them to read the sentences and correct those which are false. If they are not certain about the information, they needn't worry; they should just move on to the next statement. They can find out more during the pair work, or wait until the recording with the answers is played.

1b) Key
(Sentences 2, 3, 7, 8 and 10 are true.)
1. The capital of India is New Delhi, not Calcutta.
4. Hindi is the national language of India.
5. The currency of India is the Rupee.
6. Jawarhalal Nehru was the first prime minister of India.
9. India does not have a border with Russia.

1c)

It is best to divide this task into two distinct segments.

Learners first work in pairs and compare their answers. When they have finished, play the recording. In this phase, learners concentrate on the statements listed in 1b) and note which ones are true and which are false. The false statements should be corrected. Stop the recording after each statement so that learners can make appropriate changes.

Play the recording a second time, pausing the recording between sentences so that learners can write down other bits of information they heard. Then, ask them to call out any additional information they heard. Gather this on the board.

CD 2/32

See the tapescript on p. 195 of the Learner's Book.

Additional information:

- By 2030 India may have a larger population than China.
- About 80% of the population is Hindu.
- English is widely spoken in India.
- Mahatma Gandhi played an important role in getting independence for India.
- Mumbai is the home of India's huge film industry known as Bollywood
- India also has borders with Bangladesh, Myanmar (formerly Burma), Bhutan and Nepal.

2a)

The traveller to India will need to take quite a number of items along on the trip. The list includes a number of these items, but not all of them are depicted.
Ask learners to look at the list of words. Working individually, learners label the pictures, using words from the list.

2a) Key

1. adaptor, 2. guide book, 3. sterilisation tablets, 4. plasters, 5. repellent, 6. thermometer, 7. phrase book, 8. corkscrew

2b)

Play the recording and learners check their answers.

CD 2/33

See the tapescript on p. 195 of the Learner's Book.

2c)

Ask learners to look at the list of items again and choose three things they would definitely take along with them on a trip to India. They should also think of reasons why these things would be useful.

Learners then work in pairs and tell each other about their choices, using language similar to that in the prompt box.

3a)

Tell learners they will now hear two conversations between the receptionist at a New Delhi hotel and two hotel guests. Each of the guests needs something from the items listed in 2a).

Ask learners to close their books. Play the recording and learners note the item each person needs.

CD 2/34

See the dialogues in 3b) and the key to 3b).

3a) Key

Dialogue 1: an adaptor.
Dialogue 2: a thermometer.

3b)

First ask learners to look at the language in the bubble and elicit the meaning. Then, ask them to look at the phrases below the instruction for this step. Working individually, they use the phrases to complete the dialogues.

Play the recording again so that they can check their answers.

3b) Key

1. can I, to put, 3. You mean, 4. I could, 5. might find, 6. how can, 7. for taking, 8. so much, 9. at all, 10. let me

3c)

Working in pairs, learners practise the two dialogues. Remind them to change roles .

Now ask learners to focus on the Grammar box. Elicit the difference between the two structures, e.g. *for* is followed by a verb in the *-ing* form, whereas *to* takes the infinitive form. Learners then read the rule and fill in the missing information.

➥ things and stuff

These two words are very useful when you don't know what to call something. Note that *thing(s)* is countable *(Have you got **one of** those things ...?)* and *stuff* is uncountable *(Have you got **any of** that stuff ...?).*

3c) Key

Grammar box:
Zweck

3d)

In this activity learners work in pairs and practise describing things they need but don't know the word for. Using their dictionaries, they look for the English translation of the German word. Even if they know the English word, they should consult a dictionary. They might find more useful information there as well.

Ask learners to look at the prompt box, which indicates how the activity should be structured. Have a practice round first. Choose an unusual item yourself and ask a learner for assistance.

Learners then work in pairs and take it in turns to ask about the seven items in the list. (They are translated on p. 211 of the Learner's Book, but don't let learners look them up there before they have done the task!)

4a)

Tell learners they are going to hear a radio programme with some advice to travellers to India. Their task is to tick the things in the list that are mentioned in the interview.

First, ask learners to read the list of items. As the interview is quite long, it would be advisable to ask learners to close their books now and just listen to the recording the first time around.

Play the recording, then ask learners to open their books and look at the list of items again. They can now mark the items they are certain about. Play the recording a second time so that learners can mark any items they might have missed.

CD 2/35

See the tapescript on p. 195 of the Learner's Book.

4a) Key

the weather
what to wear
religious places
photography
shopping
the local people
the Indian way of life

4b)

This activity focuses on the interview in 4a). The list contains things that were mentioned in the interview.

Learners look at the list, then work individually and match each one with the proper definition.

4b) Key

1e, 2g, 3a, 4b, 5c, 6d, 7h, 8f

4c)

Learners listen to the recording in 4a) again for more detailed information. Ask them to read the questions. Check that they understand the phrases *advice is given concerning* and *deal with.*

Ask learners to write their answers on a piece of paper. If they can remember some of the answers, they can pencil them in before you play the recording. Allow them a bit of time to do this. More information can be added while listening.

Play the recording and use the pause button to stop the recording each time the topic changes so that learners can answer the questions as the interview progresses.

4c) Key

1. You should drink plenty of water, use sun cream and wear a hat and sunglasses when outdoors.
2. Shoes, leather items such as bags and belts might have to be left at the door.
3. One should start in government handicraft shops. The prices are fixed and the quality is guaranteed.
4. You should not shake hands when introduced to a local.
5. Don't let beggars hassle you and don't encourage them by giving them too much money.
6. 'Indian Stretchable Time' means that everything in India takes much longer than expected, so just get used to it and go with the flow if you want to enjoy your stay. Give yourself plenty of time for whatever you plan to do.

4d)

In pairs, learners now choose three or four of the topics in 4a) and write a bit of advice for tourists to their own country. When everyone has finished, ask each pair to read what they wrote.

Part B: They asked him to tell them a story

Focus
Traditional Indian stories
Writing a short story from your own country
Intonation in questions

Grammar
Reported speech: questions
- *Wh-* questions: *They asked him why ...*
- Yes/No questions: *One of them asked him if ...*
- Requests: *They asked him to ...*

1a) Revision: mixed tenses

Tell learners they are going to hear a man and a woman talking on a flight from Heathrow to New Delhi. The man, who works in the film industry, is telling the woman about India and Bollywood, the centre of the Indian film-making industry.

First, ask learners to read the questions. Then, play the recording, pausing at regular intervals to allow learners to answer the questions. They should write the answers on a piece of paper as there is no space for this in the book. If necessary, play the recording a second time.

CD 2/36
See the tapescript on pp. 195 – 196 of the Learner's Book.

1a) Key
1. She's going to meet a friend in Delhi and then go to Goa for two weeks.
2. He works with the Indian film industry.
3. The centre of the film industry.
4. It's twice as big as Hollywood and produces about 800 films a year.
5. Every day 14 million people go to the cinema in India and there is a huge foreign market as well.
6. Indians love telling stories and listening to stories.
7. Indian films always have to have a moral. There is always a strong sense of right and wrong.

➡ Bollywood
Bollywood is the informal name given to the popular Mumbai-based Hindi language film industry in India. The name is a combination of Bombay, the old name of Mumbai, and Hollywood. Sometimes the term is used incorrectly to refer to the whole of Indian cinema. It is considered to be the largest in the world in terms of number of films produced, and maybe also the number of tickets sold.

Bollywood films are often musicals. Few movies are made without at least one song-and-dance number. Indian audiences expect full value for their money and want song and dance, love interest, comedy and dare-devil thrills, all mixed up in a three-hour long movie with one intermission. These movies are called 'masala movies', after the spice mixture masala, which has everything in it.

For more information about Bollywood, visit the website:
www.bollywood.com

1b)

Ask learners to read the statements and simply mark whether they were made by the man (m) or the woman (w).

1b) Key
w: 1, 2
m: 3, 4, 5, 6

1c)

Learners now transform the direct statements in 1b) to reported speech. Start them off by getting them to look at the first item in 1b) and compare it with the prompt box at the bottom of the page.

Give the class a few minutes to look through the sentences, then call on individual learners to transform the various statement into reported speech. Get the class to agree on correct versions and write them down.

1c) Key
1. She said (that) she'd never been to India before and (that) she was really excited.
2. She said (that) she was meeting a friend in Delhi and (that) they were going to Goa for two weeks.
3. He said (that) she'd love Goa and (that) it was the perfect place for a holiday.
4. He said (that) he went to India about three times a year on business.
5. He said (that) you could never get tired of India and (that) it was an amazing place.
6. He said (that) there had always been a very strong storytelling tradition in India.

2a)

Indians love short stories and this particular one is about a popular hero called Tenali Rama and his encounter with a group of soldiers telling exciting tales of their deeds.

Ask learners to look at the picture of travellers on the road. How would they feel if they had to travel in this manner in India? Do they think it would be necessary today to travel in groups in rural India?

Ask learners to work individually and read the story.

Give them sufficient time for the reading. This is not a reading for gist task, learners must read for understanding, so they will need more time to take in the text.

In pairs, learners then choose adjectives to describe Tenali Rama and the soldiers. (The adjectives do not have to be in the text itself.) Give them a few minutes for this task, then ask them to call out the adjectives they chose and gather these on the board.

➡ Tenali Rama

Rama's full name was Tenali Ramakrishna and he lived during the reign of Krishnadeva Raya of the Vijayanagara empire (1509 – 1529). He was a court poet and court jester. He was known for his wit and prodigious poetry written in the Telugu language. His life story was made into a film in the 1950s and it is still very popular.

2a) Key

Tenali Rama (some possibilities):
small, brave, clever, intelligent, humorous, witty, weak, ragged, interesting, fast

the soldiers (some possibilities):
arrogant, brave, big, strong, self-confident, friendly

2b)

Learners now read the story again and underline all the questions that the soldiers asked Rama, then write them on a separate sheet of paper. The questions are partly in the form of reported speech and partly in direct speech.

2b) Key

1. Why are you travelling alone on such a dangerous road?
2. Do you want to join us for a while?
3. Have you got an interesting story to tell?
4. What did you do?
5. You cut off one of his fingers?
6. Why didn't you cut off his head while you had the chance?

2c)

Learners now summarise the story by matching the halves of the sentences.

2c) Key

1. One day Tenali Rama ran + into a group of soldiers on the road.
2. Their conversation turned + to stories of war.
3. One soldier told how he single-handedly + defeated a whole battalion.
4. Tenali Rama told how he had come + across a huge tent one day.
5. Inside the tent was a man who everyone was afraid + of.
6. Tenali Rama walked up to the man without + making a sound.
7. He cut off the man's finger and ran away for + dear life.

2d)

Learners now match the phrases in italics with the definitions. Note that in nos 1, 2 and 4, the definitions are in the infinitive, whereas in 2c) the verbs are in the Past simple (1, 2) and Past perfect (4). Learners should transfer the verbs in italics into the infinitive so that they match the descriptions correctly.

2d) Key

1. turn to
2. come across
3. without making a sound
4. run into
5. afraid of
6. for dear life
7. single-handedly

3a)

This pronunciation activity focuses on intonation in questions. Ask learners to read the five questions. What might the answers be?

The questions/answers fall into two categories. Can anyone say what they are? (Nos 2 and 3 can be answered with *Yes* or *No*; the others cannot.)

Make certain learners understand what their task is before playing the recording. Ask a Yes/No question, e.g. *Are you going to India this year?* and exaggerate the rising intonation. Ask learners what they heard. Some learners find it very difficult to distinguish rising and falling intonation, so you may have to repeat it a few times. Then ask an open question, e.g. *When did you go to India?* and exaggerate the falling intonation.

Now, play the recording and learners mark a rising or falling intonation. Play each sentence, stopping the recording after each one for learners to make a decision.

CD 2/37

See the five questions in 3a).

3a) Key

Up: 2, 3
Down: 1, 4, 5

3b)

Play the recording once more, pausing between each question for learners to repeat.

Now ask learners to look at the Grammar box. Focus on the first example. Is the tense shift the same as for reported speech with statements? (Yes. The Present progressive shifts to the Past progressive.)

Now focus on Yes/No questions. What is the new element here? (The tense shift is the same, but one must introduce *if* to elicit a Yes or No reply.)

Finally, look at the third section in the box. How are requests formed in reported speech? (*to* + the infinitive: *ask someone* ***to do*** *something*.)

Ask learners to read the rule and fill in the missing words.

Key

Grammar box:
Past simple; Past Perfect; Past progressive; could; would ask; if; Infinitiv (mit) to

4a)

In this activity learners make up their own stories using segments from a traditional Indian short story. The segments are in chronological order and contain enough information for learners to be able to create a story with relative ease, but without stifling their creativity.

First, ask learners to look at the segments and check that they understand the various phrases. Working in pairs, learners then build a story of their own around the segments. They can use a dictionary if they need more vocabulary.

Suggest that they start by creating the plot of the story together, orally, then make detailed notes. After that they write up their stories individually.

When learners have finished, ask them to read their versions to the class. Alternatively, you can tell learners to take their stories home and write up a more polished version and bring it to the following lesson.

4b)

After learners have read their stories to the class, play the recording of the original story. How do the learners' stories differ from it?

CD 2/38

See the tapescript on p. 196 of the Learner's Book.

4c)

This activity centres on yet another story about Tenali Rama. Ask learners to first look at the two pictures. Then, ask them to speculate on the course of the story. Who might the two people be? What is the man on the right doing? Why is he reading to the other man? What has happened in the second picture?

Play the recording and learners then decide which of the pictures best describes the story.

CD 2/39

See the tapescript on p. 196 of the Learner's Book.

4c) Key

The bottom picture

4d)

Learners now listen to the story for more detail. First, ask them to read the statements. Then, play the recording and learners mark the statements true or false.

4d) Key

True: 1, 3, 4, 6
False: 2, 5

4e)

Learners now practise direct and reported speech, using sentences from the two stories. In the first section, learners change statements from the first story from reported speech to direct speech. In the section dealing with the second story, learners change direct speech to reported speech. If they need help, they can refer back to the Grammar box on p. 132.

4e) Key

Story 1:

1. Can you help me put out the fire?
2. Are you alright?
3. Where are your hair and beard?

Story 2:

1. The poet said he would love to know Tenali Rama's opinion.
2. The poet asked Rama if he would like to hear the poems again.
3. Rama asked the poet why he wanted to read them again.

5a)

Learners now work in groups of three or four and discuss the questions. First, they talk about which of the stories they liked best, then turn their attention to traditional stories in their own country and discuss whether or not stories of this kind are important for a country's cultural identity or not and whether or not they are still popular in the country.

Allow the group work to carry on for as long as learners

are interested. If you notice that interest in the topic is not great, don't force learners to drag on, however.

5b)

In this activity, learners turn their thoughts to traditional stories from their own country. If you have a group of learners who enjoy writing and telling stories, you could ask them to work individually or in pairs. If, on the other hand, you have the impression that their interest in the topic is flagging, you could suggest a traditional story yourself and build it up with the group.

Books

This unit deals with reading and various types of literature. The first part of the unit focuses on reading in general, and books by several contemporary writers. The second part of the unit deals with one of O. Henry's short stories, 'The Last Leaf'. No new grammar is presented in the unit, but learners revise the verbs *must*, *ought to* and *should*.

Part A: You really must read it

Focus
Types of book
Books by Mark Haddon and Ian McEwan
Recommending books and other media
Favourite books

Functions
Responding to suggestions: *I could give it a go, I suppose.*

Grammar
Modal verbs *ought to, must, should* (Revision)

Pronunciation
Sounds:
/əʊ/ as in c**oa**t
/ɔː/ as in f**ou**ght

1a) Revision: questions

The learners will now hear a conversation in a bookshop between a woman who is looking for a particular book and the shop assistant.

Ask learners to read through the statements, then play the recording without a pause while learners fill in the missing information.

➡ Paul Auster

Paul Auster was born in 1957 in Newark, New Jersey and is considered by many to be one of America's finest living writers. He is particularly famous for his complex mystery novels, which are often concerned with the search for identity and personal meaning. One of his most enthralling works is 'The New York Trilogy' (1987), a trio of post-modern and experimental detective novels ('City of Glass', 'Ghosts', 'The Locked Room'). His latest work, 'Travels in the Scriptorium' (2006), has been received with varying degrees of enthusiasm.

CD 2/41

See the tapescript on p. 196 of the Learner's Book.

1a) Key

1. novel, 2. yesterday, 3. Friday, 4. Saturday, 5. 9 a.m.

1b)

Learners now work individually and reconstruct the questions from the dialogue.

1b) Key

1. Have you got the new Paul Auster novel?
2. When do you think you'll get more copies?
3. Do you want us to give you a call when we get some?
4. What time do you open on Saturdays?
5. Do you want me to put a copy aside for you?

1c) Revision: Reported speech

In this activity, learners revise reported questions by transforming the direct questions in 1b) to the reported question form. Before learners go about the task, you might want to revise this point of grammar with them. Ask them to look at the Grammar box on p.132. Elicit the basic rules.

Learners then work individually and write the reported questions. Remind them to look very carefully at the direct questions and consider all the changes of pronouns necessary to create a grammatically-correct version in the reported questions.

While learners are working, write each of the direct questions on the board, leaving plenty of space to add the reported versions. When they have finished, ask individual learners to read out their questions. Write these on the board so that it will be obvious to learners which changes are required.

1c) Key

1. She asked him if he/they had got the new Paul Auster novel.
2. She asked him when he thought he/they would get more copies.
3. He asked her if she wanted them to give her a call when they got some.
4. She asked him what time they opened on Saturdays.
5. He asked her if she wanted him to put her a copy aside.

2a)

In this activity learners categorise various types of books into fiction and non-fiction.

First, read the list of words and ask learners to repeat them after you. Pay particular attention to stress, which is not always what German speakers would expect: *atlas, manual, poetry anthology, romantic novel, horror.*

Learners then work individually and categorise the words.

2a) Key
Fiction:
short stories, poetry anthology, romantic novel, crime novel, horror novel

Non-fiction:
atlas, manual, self-help book, travel guide, cookery book

2b)
Learners now think of more types of books. They can do this activity either in pairs or individually, using a dictionary if necessary. Give them about five minutes to write their lists, then ask each learner in turn to call out one of their items, saying whether it is fiction or non-fiction. Write them on the board, putting them into the proper category.

2a) Key
Learners' own ideas.

Some possibilities:
Non-fiction: history books, DIY books, gardening books, handicraft books, health books, catalogues, song books, biographies, autobiographies, religious books, dictionaries, encyclopedias
Fiction: science fiction novels, fairy tales, historical novels

3a)
This pronunciation activity contrasts the differences between the diphthong /əʊ/ and the /ɔː/ sound.

Ask learners to look at the words in the lists. Pronounce each of the words slowly and carefully and ask learners to describe the differences they hear. In the diphthong /əʊ/ there is a noticeable gliding from the /ə/ (schwa) to the /ʊ/. Both phonemes require noticeable rounding of the lips for proper pronunciation.

Now ask learners to look at the list of words, paying attention to the underlined sounds. Don't read the words aloud at this point, however. Play the recording, stopping after each word. Learners say the word to themselves, then add it to the correct list. Check by asking learners to call out the words, saying which list they put them in.

CD 2/42
awful, romantic, ought, short, poetry, vocabulary, story, thought, open, sold

3a) Key
List 1:
coat, romantic, poetry, vocabulary, open, sold

List 2:
fought, awful, ought, short, story, thought

3b)
Play the recording again, pausing after each word. Ask learners to repeat the word in chorus.

3c)
Read out each of the sentences yourself, then move quickly round the group, asking each person to repeat it.

4a)
Ask learners to look at the picture and the bubble, and speculate about what they are going to hear.

Tell them they are going to hear two dialogues, with people talking about different books, and should make notes on what they hear. They might not recognise the author's name or the titles of the books, but this needn't worry them, as in real life they would have the opportunity to ask about them again.

Play the first dialogue and learners write down as much as they can. Give them time to complete their notes, then carry on to the second dialogue.

CD 2/43
See the dialogues in 4c) and the key to 4c).

4b)
Learners now compare their notes with a partner, add any further information and discuss any discrepancies of detail they might discover. Give them a few minutes to do this, then play the dialogues again so they can check their work.

4c)
Ask learners to look at the list of questions. Elicit the meaning of each. Working individually, they complete the dialogues using the questions in the list. They can write the numbers of the missing questions in the brackets while they are sorting them out, then write them out in full in the appropriate gap.

⚠
Note that two of the questions are very similar:
3. *What's it called?*
4. *what was it called?*

➡ **Mark Haddon**
Mark Haddon was born in 1962 in Northampton and has been writing successful children's books since 1987. His first novel, 'The Curious Incident of the Dog in the Night-Time', was hugely successful. It is the first book to have been published in two imprints, one for children and one for adults. The book has won many awards, including the 2003 Whitbread Book of the Year.

➡ Ian McEwan
McKewan was born in 1948 in Aldershot, Hampshire. His novel 'Atonement' was shortlisted for the Booker Prize for Fiction and the Whitbread Novel Award and won the WH Smith Literary Award. In this novel he tells the story of Briony, a young girl and aspiring writer, and the consequences of the discovery she makes about Robbie, a young man destined to play a part in the Dunkirk evacuations.

4c) Key
Dialogue 1:
what was it called?
Why not?
What's it called?

Dialogue 2:
Who's it by?
And what's it about?
In what way?
So how does he solve a murder?

4d)
Ask learners to look at the six expressions listed here. Working individually, they read the dialogues again and match the phrases in italics with the expressions in the list. Point out that they may not be identical in meaning, but do convey the same sense.

4d) Key
1. put it down
2. I don't want to give too much away.
3. give it a go
4. plot
5. latest
6. I'm not really a fan.

4e)
Before learners begin this activity, ask them to look at the Grammar box, which revises some ways of making recommendations.

Learners now work individually and think of musicals, CDs, TV programmes or books that they like a lot. Ask them to think about why they would recommend them to someone. They should also think for a moment about what they are about.

Learners then work in pairs and talk to each other about the things they have chosen.

5a)
This activity concentrates on books and learners' reading habits. Ask learners to read the questions, then discuss them in pairs. Allow them plenty of time for the discussion.

When the discussion has ended, call on various learners to make one statement about what their partner said. They should do this using reported speech.

5b)
Learners now redraft the questions in preparation for an interview about film preferences. Working individually, learners write at least five questions they would like to ask a partner about their film interests.

5c)
Working in pairs, learners interview each other, using the questions they have written.

When the interview activity has ended, ask each learner to report something about the person interviewed. Again, this should be done using reported speech.

Part B: The Last Leaf

Focus
O. Henry's short story 'The Last Leaf'
Reading, listening, speaking and writing tasks relating to the story

Functions
Giving opinions: *I really like the way the story ...; I thought (the story) was a bit silly because ...; The only part I didn't think was so good was ...; What I liked most about the story was ...; I wasn't really convinced by the ...*
Agreeing: *I agree with most of what you say but ...; That's exactly what I feel, too.*
Disagreeing: *I don't really agree with anything you say; I take your point, but I'm afraid I don't agree completely.*

1a) Revision: making recommendations

Ask learners to think of two books and two films they really enjoyed, then write down the titles.

1a) Key
Learners' own choices

1b)

Working in groups of three or four, learners tell each other about their choices. They should use the verbs *ought to* and *must* to recommend their choices.

1c)

Ask learners to look at the list, which focuses on various aspects of a story. Each learner decides which of the things on the list is most important to them. They can add something if they feel it is missing from the list.

Ask learners to say which of the things are most important for them personally.

1c) Key
Learners' own choices

2a)

The remainder of this unit deals with 'The Last Leaf', a famous short story by the American author O. Henry. The original story has been edited for teaching purposes.

Before starting the task, ask if anyone has read any of O. Henry's stories or knows anything about him. Tell them to look later at the Reading for Fun text in the Practice section, p.147, for biographical information about this interesting literary personality.

The story has been divided into four sections, alternating between reading and listening comprehension. Each of the four sections will be approached in several different ways, allowing the learners to grasp the content of the story in a systematic and controlled manner without being overwhelmed by the length of the text.

The tasks are well structured, so there is no need to offer information beyond what is in the activity itself. At the end of each of the sections, just make certain that learners have understood the plot up to that point.

Start by asking learners to look at the six statements dealing with the characters in the story and the main elements of the plot. Before they begin, remind them that it is not important at this point to understand every word in the text. They will be fully able to answer the questions even if some of the vocabulary is unclear.

Tell learners to read the text carefully and give them sufficient time to do so. Don't set a time limit. Just be watchful yourself, noticing when most people seem to be finished. When they have finished reading the text, ask them to mark the statements true or false. They should refer back to the text and underline the statement confirming their choice.

2a) Key
True: 1, 2, 3
False: 4, 5, 6

2b)

Learners now focus their attention on fifteen new lexical items, all of which are in italics in the text. Ask learners to look through the text and circle all the words in italics. They now choose five that they really want to check the meaning of, and look them up in their dictionaries.

When everyone has finished, call on various learners to mention one of their choices and the meaning they found. If, at the end of the activity, some words have not been discussed, elicit the meaning from the class.

At this point, ask learners if there are sections of the text they do not understand. If so, clarify difficult points before moving on to the next section.

2b) Key
Learners' own choice of words from 2a)

3a)

The next segment of the story is presented as a recorded dialogue with a listening comprehension task. Tell learners they will now hear the continuation of the story, which is a conversation between Mr Behrman and Sue. Sue has gone downstairs to talk to him about Joanna.

Ask learners to close their books and just listen. Play the recording, then ask various learners to say what they think Mr Behrmann's plan is.

CD 2/44
See the dialogue in 3b) and the key to 3b).

3a) Key
Learners' own ideas

3b)
Now, ask learners to look at the phrases below the instruction. Working individually, they write the phrases in the correct places in the dialogue.

3b) Key
1. you look as if
2. you can tell me
3. the most stupid idea
4. I'm not joking
5. my great work of art
6. let me get on

3c)
Play the recording and learners check their answers.

4
The next segment of the story is presented as a reading comprehension text. Before beginning with this section, you could ask learners to speculate on the outcome of the story.

Ask them to look through the four statements and then read the text. Again, remind them that it is not necessary to understand every word. Give them enough time to read the text carefully and correct the sentences. Ask them to underline the relevant section in the text.

Again, ask learners if there are any segments of the text they have not understood. If so, explain them or ask other learners to do so.

4 Key
1. The next morning the last leaf was still there.
2. The doctor said that Joanna's chances were 50/50.
3. The doctor was going to visit Mr Behrman downstairs.
4. The doctor thought there was no chance for him.

5a)
Now ask learners to speculate on what Sue is going to tell Joanna. Allow learners to give their views, but don't give the ending away. Carry on to the listening comprehension, where learners find out how the story ends.

5b)
Play the recording. How many guessed the right ending?

CD 2/45
See the tapescript on pp. 196 – 197 of the Learner's Book.

5c)
Learners now listen to the ending again for more detail. Ask them to read the questions, then play the recording again. Learners should note down their answers as the recording progresses.

5c) Key
1. He was ill for two days.
2. They found him in his room downstairs.
3. They found a lamp and ladder and brushes.
4. There was green and yellow paint on them.
5. He had painted the ivy leaf.

6a)
In this activity, learners give their opinion of the story. First, ask them to look at the two prompt boxes. These feature three different ways of expressing one's opinions, agreeing and disagreeing. In each of the boxes, the language is presented with increasingly complex structures.

Ask learners to focus their attention on the first box and read the phrases. Each of the phrases also deals with an aspect of the story that one could discuss, e.g. the part one liked best; a part that wasn't so good; something that wasn't particularly convincing; something that seemed a bit silly. Ask learners to underline these aspects.

Next, ask learners to turn their attention to the second box, which features agreeing / disagreeing. Ask them to read the individual statements. Then, ask them to focus on *I don't really agree with anything you say* and *I take your point but I'm afraid I don't agree completely.* Both sentences express disagreement, but are they equally polite? (The more difficult structure is certainly more polite than the less difficult one.)

Learners now work in pairs and discuss their opinions of the story. They might cover some of the topics they underlined in the first prompt box, but they could discuss their opinions about other aspects of the story as well.

6b)
This writing task is designed as a pair activity. Learners have four different topics from which they can choose.

The first topic is very open, as learners have no idea

what star signs the three belong to. They would also have to create characteristics belonging to the signs they chose for each person. This would be a topic requiring a great deal of creative input. The second topic is more of a character study and description of what Joanna might have learned from the experience. The third topic might possibly involve an expression of Joanna's gratitude to Mr Behrman, as well as an acknowledgement of her own foolishness. The fourth topic would, of course, require a well-defined message.

Ask the pairs to choose a topic to write about and note the points they would like to cover in their text. Then they set about writing it. When everyone has finished, ask each pair to read their texts. Collect the individual texts and correct them at home. Deal with any serious mistakes as part of a general feedback in the next lesson.

The past

The first part of the unit focuses on the Channel Islands and a woman who talks about growing up there. The second part of the unit features a text about Isabella Lucy Bird, a remarkable woman of the Victorian era. The Grammar focus is the third conditional, and the verbs *used to* and *remember*. Learners write a short biography of a person they admire.

Part A: My father used to take me for walks

Focus
The Channel Islands
Memories and childhood

Grammar
Verbs
used to: My father used to take me for walks; We didn't use to learn much French at school.
remember + verb + *-ing: I remember sitting on my father's knee.*

Pronunciation
used to

1a) Revision: Past simple and Present Perfect

This task introduces the topic of places where one has lived and revises the use of two major tenses.

Ask learners to read the statements, each of which is a description about where one has lived in the course of one's life. Learners select the statement that most closely describes their own personal situation.

1b)

Learners now walk around and talk to others about the statement they have chosen. The partners should ask for details.

Let the activity carry on until learners have talked to three or four other people.

Ask various learners to comment on one of their conversations. They should report the partner's information using indirect speech.

1c)

Tell learners they will hear a recording of a man talking about where he now lives and where he used to live. Ask them to read the text, then close their books and just listen to the interview.

Learners then open their books. Give them a moment to fill in any of the information they might have retained from the recording. Play it again, stopping periodically so that learners can complete the rest of the text.

At this point, learners might expect/ask for more information about the Channel Islands. Tell them they can find many interesting facts in the Reading for Fun text in the Practice section, p. 152.

CD 2/46
See the tapescript on p. 197 of the Learner's Book.

1c) Key
1. Oxford, 2. four, 3. thirty, 4. aunt and uncle, 5. nice beaches (and things), 6. twenty, 7. English

2a)

Learners now find out more about Jersey in a rather long interview with a woman who has lived there all her life.

Ask learners to look at the language in the bubble. What do they think *I used to* (walk past them) could mean?

Learners now read the statements, then tick the ones they think might be true.

2b)

Now, play the recording and learners tick the boxes true or false. If necessary, play the recording a second time.

Did anyone predict all five statements correctly? Did they think any of the statements were unusual?

⚠
The first item *(She has never left Jersey)* comes up early on in the recording but learners then have to listen for quite a while before no. 2 *(She went to an-all girls school)* is mentioned.

CD 2/47
See the tapescript on p. 197 of the Learner's Book.

2b) Key
True: 1, 2, 3
False: 4, 5

2c)

Ask learners to look at the four pictures, each of which illustrates something Vera mentions in the interview. Learners listen to the interview again and put the pictures in the order they are mentioned. (They number the left-hand box in each picture. The right box will be used in the next activity.)

2c) Key
(From left to right)
Top row: 1, 2
Bottom row: 3, 4

2d)

First ask learners to look at the Grammar box at the bottom of the page, which features the verb *used to.* How is the structure formed? (*used to* + the infinitive). Get learners to read the German explanation at the top of the right-hand column.

Learners now read the eight statements, which Vera made in the interview. Ask for a translation of each. Learners then work individually and match four of the statements with the appropriate pictures in 2c).

⚠
Learners who have had English before may want to use the phrase *in former times* instead of *used to*. This would not be correct here. *In former times* is used to refer to another era, to a distant past such as the Middle Ages.

2d) Key
1e, 2h, 3g, 4b

3a)

Ask learners to read the phrases. Point out that *didn't used to go* (which is split on the page) belongs together. If learners fail to notice this, they will have difficulty completing the sentences correctly.

Learners then work individually and complete the sentences. (They should ignore the brackets at the end of the sentences, which are used for the task in 3c).

3a) Key
1. used to be
2. used to go
3. use to eat
4. didn't use to go
5. used to watch
6. used to do

3b)

The focus in this step is the pronunciation of *used to*, in particular:
- the unvoiced *s* (as opposed to the voiced *s* in the verb *to use*);
- the weakform of *to*: /tə/.

Play the recording so that learners can check their answers to 3a). Then play it again, pausing after each sentence. Get learners to repeat the sentence in chorus.

CD 2/48
See the six sentences in 3a).

3c)

Learners now think back to the time when they were teenagers. They read the sentences in 3a) again and tick (in the brackets) those statements which are true for them.

After they have ticked the sentences, ask them to look at the prompt box and read the examples. Note that each includes the verb *used to*.

In groups of four or five, learners compare the things they ticked in 3a). They will have an opportunity to talk about their teenage years in more detail in 3e).

3d)

Choosing verbs from the list, learners write down six things they used to do.

3e)

Ask learners to look at the prompt box. Focus their attention on the first example. What would the complete sentence be? *(And are used to eat loads of chocolate.)*

Learners again work in groups of four or five and exchange more information about their way of life as teenagers.

4a)

In this activity, attention is shifted to remembering things, to memories and reminders.

First, ask learners to look at the pictures and decide what the various things all have in common. Then get them to talk about each picture, mentioning the purpose of each. Gather essential vocabulary on the board, e.g. *remind, remember, memory.*

4a) Key
Learners' own ideas

4b)

Ask learners to look at the words in the list. Elicit the differences between *memorable, memorial, memory.*

Working individually, learners complete the sentences about the pictures in 4a).

4b) Key
1. forget, 2. remember, 3. memory, 4. remind, 5. memorial, 6. memorable

4c)

Learners now personalise the vocabulary and mention things they do to help them remember something.

4c) Key
Learners' own strategies

5a)

In this activity the emphasis is shifted to the verb *remember*.

Ask learners to read the sentences in the prompt box. What do they notice about the verbs that follow *remember*? (They take the *-ing* form). Ask learners if they can think of other verbs which require the same structure, e.g. *like, hate, love, enjoy*. Then, ask them to complete the rule with any additional verbs they can think of.

Learners now read the sentences and mention whether any of them are true for them. If not, they can use the structure to make a true statement about themselves.

⚠
The examples in the prompt box all refer to things in the past. Note that *remember* can also be followed by a verb in the infinitive, e.g. *I must* ***remember to go*** *to the post office*. In this case it refers to something which has not yet been done.

5a) Key
Grammar box:
remember, love, hate, like, enjoy

5b)

In this activity learners prepare a one or two-minute talk about their childhood memories. They can use the ideas in the list or talk about other memorable events.

Next ask learners to look at the list and decide what they would like to talk about. Remind them that the time is short, so they should concentrate on one or two things that they can talk about in detail.

Now ask learners to look at the prompt box, which features good openers for their talk. They will probably find it easiest to choose one of these, then carry on from there.

Tell learners they can make notes, but shouldn't write out a full text and read it to the class. The talk should flow naturally from one point to the next and the notes should just remind the speaker of the points to be covered.

5c)

When learners have finished their preparation, they take it in turns to give their talks. Don't be too strict about the time limit; it is difficult to be exact without doing a practice run first.

During the talks you should make notes on grammar weaknesses but don't comment on each individual talk. When everyone has finished, give general feedback, highlighting mistakes without mentioning names.

5c) Key
Learners' own talks

Part B: If her father hadn't given her £100

Focus
Isabella Lucy Bird, a Victorian explorer
Personal events and results
Writing a biography

Grammar
The third conditional: *If Isabella had been healthier, her doctor wouldn't have told her to travel; She might have found it easier to get to sleep at night if her back operation had been successful.*

1a) Revision: the verb *used to*

Ask learners to look at the pictures, both of which depict young women in Victorian Britain. Before beginning the activity, you might ask learners which period of time is covered by the term Victorian Britain.

Ask learners to look at the list which covers various aspects of life. Then, ask them to look at the prompt box, which features statements with the verb *used to.*

Working individually, learners write a sentence for each of the various aspects of life listed. Each should include the use of *used to.*

➡ Victorian Britain
This period covers the time of the reign of Queen Victoria (1837 – 1901). Queen Victoria was born in 1819 and succeeded her uncle, William IV, at the age of 18. She married Prince Albert of Saxe-Coburg-Gotha. Her reign dominated the rest of the century. Achievements during her reign include: the Great Exhibition at the Crystal Palace in 1851; a growing interest in the arts and sciences; the founding of some of Britain's greatest public museums and institutional reform leading to a more constitutional monarchy. The most notable achievement was probably the expansion of the British Empire, in particular in India, Australia, Canada and parts of Africa and the South Pacific.

1b)

This activity can be done with the class. Chair the discussion yourself and work through the various topics listed.

2a)

The following series of tasks concerns Isabella Lucy Bird, an extremely independent and adventurous Victorian woman who refused to be held back either by her own physical limitations or the limitations placed on women by society. The reading text is a biography which contains much detail about her life.

Start by asking learners to look at the title, 'An Independent Spirit'. Elicit the meaning, then run through the ten questions with the class and check that they understand them.

The text should be read in two phases. Learners should first just skim through it for the gist, taking in general information about Isabella Lucy Bird and her adventures. They then read the text a second time for detail, underlining the information they will need to answer the questions.

Finally, learners answer the questions by noting Bird's age at the time of each event. This will require not only careful reading, but a bit of calculation, too, as most of the events are mentioned with dates.

Remind learners before they begin that there might be some words they are not familiar with. These will not be a hindrance for the completion of the task, however. A later task deals with new vocabulary.

2a) Key

1. 19	3. 25	5. 47	7. 50	9. 70
2. 23	4. 40	6. 42	8. 55	10. 73

2b)

Ask learners to look at the true/false statements. Which of them are they already sure about? Let them read the text again to check. Remind them to underline the segment of the text which confirms their choice.

2b) Key
True: 1, 3, 5, 6
False: 2, 4, 7, 8

2c)

Learners match the sentences halves. (Don't answer any questions about grammar yet.)

When they have finished, ask learners to look at the Grammar Box in the right-hand column. This focuses on the third conditional, which is used to speculate about things that could have happened in the past but didn't.

Ask learners to read the first example. How is it constructed? (*if* + Past Perfect, *would have* + past participle). Now ask them to look at the second example. How does it differ in structure from the first example? (use of *might* and the order of the clauses.) What about the punctuation in the two examples? (If the relative clause comes first, a comma is used to separate it from the main clause.)

Learners complete the sentence below the box. Let them check the Grammar section (p. 169) if they are uncertain.

2c) Key
Sentences:
2a, 4b, 5c, 6d, 1e, 3f

Grammar box:
Past Perfect
would (oder) might
Present Perfect
sie in der Vergangenheit liegt
(und dort tatsächlich nicht erfüllt wurde).

2d)

Learners work in groups of three or four and discuss the questions about Isabella Bird's success and related topics. They should appoint a group secretary to note down some of the ideas discussed. When they have finished their group discussion, ask them to get together with another group and compare their answers.

3a)

Ask learners to look at the prompt box, then write two or three sentences about things that could have happened in their own lives, but didn't. They should use the third conditional for this.

3b)

Learners now take it in turns to read one of their statements to the class. Other members of the class ask questions about the events mentioned. In order to give everyone an opportunity to make a statement and ask others about their statements, individual utterances should be limited to one statement or question.

4a)

In this activity, learners again focus their attention on the text about Isabella Bird.

Learners read the definitions in the list, then look back at the words that are underlined in the text and match them with the appropriate definition.

4a) Key
1. travel, 2. set off, 3. get away, 4. get (got) back, 5. trip, 6. explorer, 7. foreign, 8. go abroad

4b)

In this activity learners work individually and complete the questions using the words from 4a).

4b) Key
1. travel, 2. trips, 3. foreign, 4. set off, 5. get back, 6. go abroad, 7. get away, 8. explorer

4c)

Working in pairs learners and discuss the questions in 4b).

5

In this task, learners write a biography of a person they admire or are interested in. It should be short und succinct, covering only essential details. They can invent details if necessary.

First, discuss the task with the class. Ask them to skim over the biography of Isabella Bird again. What does it cover?
- name of the person and date of birth and death;
- why the person is famous/their achievements;
- further interesting details.

Learners should cover the same things in their biographies, and include a statement as to why they admire the person they chose, or find them particularly interesting.

Learners work individually. (Suggest they write their biography on a separate piece of paper rather than in the book.) Remind them to sketch their biography out first in note form. Circulate and help with grammar and vocabulary as necessary.

When everyone has finished, ask learners to read their biographies out to the class.

See you!

In this last unit, learners revise grammar, vocabulary, and functional language that has been covered in Fairway 3. The unit also features ideas about how to keep up one's English after the course.

The best of luck!

Focus
Vocabulary revision
Grammar revision
Functional exchanges in common situations
Common words in English
Keeping up your English
Saying goodbye

Functions
Suggesting: *We must keep in touch.*
Expressing an intention: *I'll phone you.*
Wishing someone well: *The best of luck; I'd like to wish you all the best; Look after yourself.*
Greeting: *Give my regards to ...*

1a) Revision: core vocabulary

This activity revises basic word fields. Learners work individually and add one more word to each of the groups.

When learners have finished, ask them to call out the words they added to each group.

1a) Key
Some possibilities:
1. fall or autumn
2. science fiction, adventure, crime
3. cotton, rubber
4. cool
5. excited, sad, depressed, interested
6. friendly, helpful, generous, loving
7. novel, poetry, gardening book
8. computer, mobile, digital camera

1b)

Learners now work in pairs and think of different groups of words and write them down. Each group should include three words.

When they have finished the pair work, they exchange lists with another pair and add to the list they have been given.

Ask each pair to read out one of the lists they have completed, then call for additions from others in the class.

1b) Key
Learners' own ideas

2a)

Tell learners they are going to hear two dialogues where people say goodbye and talk about forthcoming changes in their lives.

Ask learners to read the options, then play the recording. Pause between dialogues so that learners can make their choices.

CD 2/50
See the dialogues in 2b) and the key to 2b).

2a) Key
1b, 2a

2b)

Ask learners to look at the phrases below the instruction. Working individually, they use them to complete the dialogue.

2c)

Play the recording again and learners check their work.

2b) Key
Dialogue 1:
1. must keep in touch
2. come and see us
3. you can be sure
4. have to say goodbye

Dialogue 2:
5. you know what they say
6. I know it
7. wish you all the best
8. the best of luck.

2d)

Learners now refer back to the dialogue and look for the English equivalent of the German expressions.

2d) Key
1. I'm going to miss you.
2. Give my regards to
3. look after yourself
4. you know what they say
5. the best of luck

2e)

Learners now practise the dialogues in pairs. Remind them to change roles during the practice.

3a)

In this activity learners speculate on the ten most common words in the English language. This should help to focus their attention more closely on those many small, perhaps uninteresting-looking words -articles, pronouns, prepositions, etc. – that are nonetheless essential to communication.

⚠

The list of twenty words is based on a study of British, American and Australian English (http://www.world-english.org/english500.htm).
Any such list will of course depend on the sample of language studied, along with other factors such as whether the sample is of written or spoken language, the region or country that the speaker comes from and their age and educational level.

3a) Key
In descending order of frequency:
the, of, to, and, a, in, is, it, you, that

3b)

Learners now consider another list of words and decide which five of them could be amongst the 100 most common words in English.

3b) Key
The study mentioned in 3a) lists the following words: can, did, down, like, way

4a)

In this task, learners create mini-dialogues by finding pairs of sentences: statements/responses and questions/answers.

Working individually, they match the pairs up by writing the number of the sentence into the appropriate box.

4a) Key
5a, 3b, 1c, 4d, 9e, 12f, 8g, 10h, 11i, 2j, 7k, 6l

4b)

Working in pairs, learners now choose two of the mini-dialogues in 4a) and add a couple of lines to them. Remind them to write the dialogues down.

4c)

The pairs take it in turns to act out their dialogues. When everyone has had a turn, vote for the best dialogue(s).

5a)

In the following series of tasks learners consider what they can do to keep up their English after the course has ended. The goal here is to arrive at a concrete plan of action that can be carried through successfully.

Ask learners to read through the eight ideas. Then, working individually, they number the ideas according to their relevance for themselves. The best idea should receive a 1; the worst idea receives an 8.

When everyone has finished, go through the list asking for a show of hands for each suggestion, e.g. *Who thinks number 1 is the best idea?* You could draw up a chart on the board to show which of the suggestions seem most likely to be helpful.

5b)

Learners now work individually and add anything else to the list that they can think of.

When everyone has finished, ask learners to call out their ideas and gather them on the board.

5c)

Learners now walk around and discuss their responses and ideas. They should make a list of people who would be interested in doing some of these activities with them. Not only should they note down the names of the people, but they should also try to make a date to get together and actually get started. Each of the suggestions requires action of some sort, from regularly working with someone else to looking for courses where one can continue English.

When learners have finished talking to each other, call on each one to make a statement about his or her future course of action.

6

Learners now say goodbye to you and the others in the class.

Ask them to look at the phrases in the prompt box. If they like, they can write them down on a slip of paper. Then ask everyone to stand up and, using appropriate phrases from the list, say goodbye to each person.

CEF Checklist
On pages 163-164 of the Learners' Book you will find a self-evaluation checklist for Level B1 of the Common European Framework of Reference for Languages. The checklist serves two purposes. Firstly, it informs you as a teacher about the content of the book, with reference to the descriptors for communicative competence contained in the CEF document. Secondly, it allows learners to evaluate their own progress and determine what language material has been successfully mastered and what may require further work.

Throughout the book, learners have been monitoring

their progress through the Mein Lernfortschritt sections, which come at the end of each Self-check. The self-evaluation gives them an additional opportunity to assess their progress in more detail and by doing so, pave the way for setting realistic learning goals for the future.

Language portfolio
Should your group be working with a Language Portfolio, this self-assessment is an integral part of the portfolio work. If you have not yet begun work with a Language Portfolio, but would like further information about it, visit the comprehensive web site of the Council of Europe (http://culture2.coe.int/portfolio) Here you will find a wealth of information about the Common European Framework as well as the Language Portfolio, an important element of the CEF.

B1 Certificate in English exam
Now that learners have completed Fairway 3 they have covered the language material required to take the **B1 Certificate in English** exam, an internationally recognized language exam developed by the Weiterbildungstestsysteme (WBS) in Frankfurt. For further information regarding this exam, which can be downloaded and implemented directly in the classroom, you might like to visit their website, http://www.telc.net

Dialogue 1

□ Hello. I haven't seen you for ages. How are you?

○ Fine, thanks. And you?

□ Me too. So, what have you been up to?

○ Not a lot. Well, I went on holiday to Italy.

□ Wonderful! Was it good?

○ It was great. We had a fantastic time.

Dialogue 2

△ Have we met before?

▼ I don't think so. I'm Natasha, I'm a friend of Michael's.

△ Hi, Natasha, my name's Sonia. Nice to meet you.

▼ Nice to meet you, too. Do you know many people here?

△ No, I don't. Do you know anyone?

▼ Yes, one or two people. Let me introduce you to them.

Find someone who …

1. is not from this town / city. *(Where …?)*

   Person 1: ______________________________

   Person 2: ______________________________

2. hasn't got a car. *(Have …?)*

   Person 1: ______________________________

   Person 2: ______________________________

3. doesn't smoke. *(Do …?)*

   Person 1: ______________________________

   Person 2: ______________________________

4. speaks more than one language. *(Do …?)*

   Person 1: ______________________________

   Person 2: ______________________________

5. prefers theatre to cinema. *(Do …?)*

   Person 1: ______________________________

   Person 2: ______________________________

6. was in this class last semester. *(Were …?)*

   Person 1: ______________________________

   Person 2: ______________________________

7. travelled somewhere last year. *(Did …?)*

   Person 1: ______________________________

   Person 2: ______________________________

8. has learned English for more than two years. *(How …?)*

   Person 1: ______________________________

   Person 2: ______________________________

Keep up your English

☐ Check the tips in your book.

☐ Call other people from the course – and speak English!

☐ Make 'word cards': Write an English word on one side, the German word on the other. Test yourself!

☐ Listen to the dialogues at home or in your car. Practise them.

☐ Invite friends who speak English. Have a good time together speaking English!

☐ Write all the speech bubbles from the book onto small cards. Practise them.

☐ Write letters or e-mails in English to someone in another country.

☐ Speak English with native speakers.

☐ Learn roles from the dialogues by heart.

☐ Write down vocab that is important to you (My vocab).

☐ Write all the texts you have written in the last semester in your own scrapbook: (My English Portfolio)

✂ -

Keep up your English

☐ Check the tips in your book.

☐ Call other people from the course – and speak English!

☐ Make 'word cards': Write an English word on one side, the German word on the other. Test yourself!

☐ Listen to the dialogues at home or in your car. Practise them.

☐ Invite friends who speak English. Have a good time together speaking English!

☐ Write all the speech bubbles from the book onto small cards. Practise them.

☐ Write letters or e-mails in English to someone in another country.

☐ Speak English with native speakers.

☐ Learn roles from the dialogues by heart.

☐ Write down vocab that is important to you (My vocab).

☐ Write all the texts you have written in the last semester in your own scrapbook: (My English Portfolio)

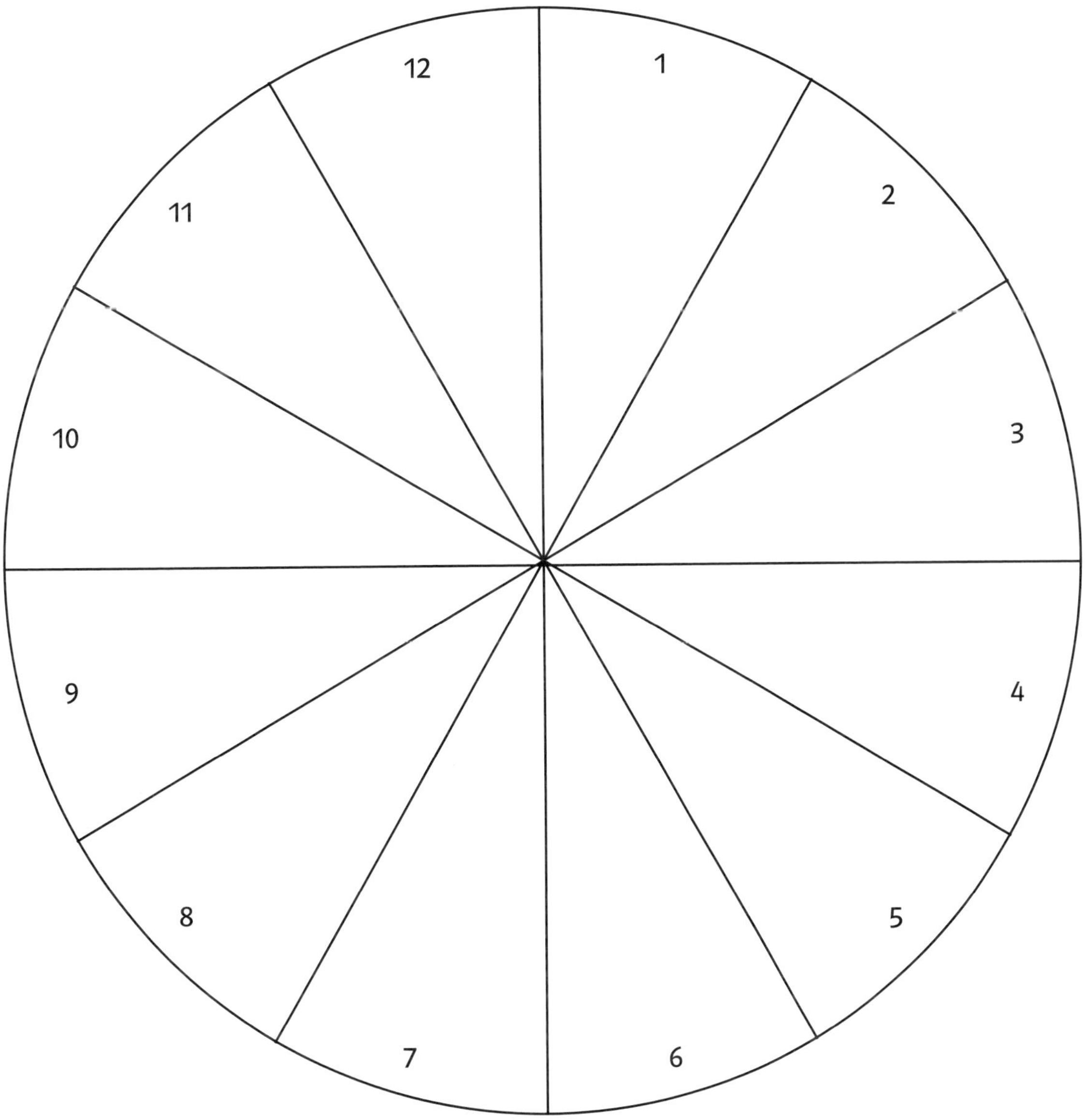

Questions

1. Name three things you can do on holiday.
2. Tell the others about your favourite dish. What has it got in it?
3. Describe your favourite piece of clothing.
4. Someone has just given you €100. What would you buy with it?
5. Name one job you would like to have and one job you would not like to have.
6. Describe a friend or someone in your family. How old is the person? What does he/she look like? Why do you like this person?
7. Name three things you always take with you on holiday.
8. How did you celebrate your last birthday?
9. Name one thing you would like to learn and say why you want to learn it.
10. Where did you spend your worst holiday? Why was it bad?
11. How are you going to spend next weekend?
12. Name three parts of the body.

Anna Pavlova (1881-1931)

Russian ballet dancer who became world famous for the romantic roles she danced. For most of her career she danced at the Mariinsky Theatre in St. Petersburg.

Liam Neeson (1957-)

Irish actor, now living in New York. His most notable role to date is that of Oscar Schindler in the film *Schindler's List.*

Oscar Niemeyer (1907 -)

Brazilian architect who is considered one of the most important names in international modern architecture. His creations, which are located all over the world, are famous for their dynamic forms and beautiful curves.

Sinead O'Connor (1966 -)

Popular, but controversial, Irish singer whose songs can be characterised as 'roots reggae'. Reggae is a music genre developed in Jamaica, and the term can be used to apply to most types of Jamaican music. Reggae is often associated wit the Rastafari movement, a religious movement which influenced many reggae singers.

Florence Nightingale (1829-1910)

Social reformer most known for her work in Turkey during the Crimean War. She fought for the reform of hygiene standards in military hospitals and founded the Nightingale School & Home for nurses at St. Thomas' Hospital in London. She was also active on behalf of women's rights and for the removal of restrictions that prevented women having careers.

Oscar Wilde (Oscar Fingal O'Flahertie Wills Wilde – 1854-1900)

Irish writer. He is regarded as one of the greatest playwrights of the Victorian era, his best-loved play being, perhaps, *The Importance of Being Ernest.* His only novel, *The Picture of Dorian Gray*, has become a literary classic.

Hillary Clinton (1947-)

Elected United States Senator for New York in 2001. She is married to Bill Clinton, the 42nd President of the United States and was First Lady of the United States from 1993-2001. She is well-known for her liberal views on social issues such as education and health.

Donald Trump (1946 -)

Business executive, founder and CEO of Trump Organization of the USA, which is mainly involved in the premium American real estate segment. He has gained much notoriety over the years for his extravagant lifestyle.

Lost Property

Name ______________________________

Contact Number ____________________

Lost item: ____

Description of item (colour, material, contents, etc.) __________________________________

____

Where was it lost? ____

When was it lost? ____

✂- -

Lost Property

Name ______________________________

Contact Number ____________________

Lost item: ____

Description of item (colour, material, contents, etc.) __________________________________

____

Where was it lost? ____

When was it lost? ____

✂- -

Lost Property

Name ______________________________

Contact Number ____________________

Lost item: ____

Description of item (colour, material, contents, etc.) __________________________________

____

Where was it lost? ____

When was it lost? ____

My speciality

From the kitchen of

____

Name of dish

____

Serves

____

Ingredients

____

____

____

____

____

Preparation

____

____

____

____

____

____

____

____

____

____

____

____

____

____

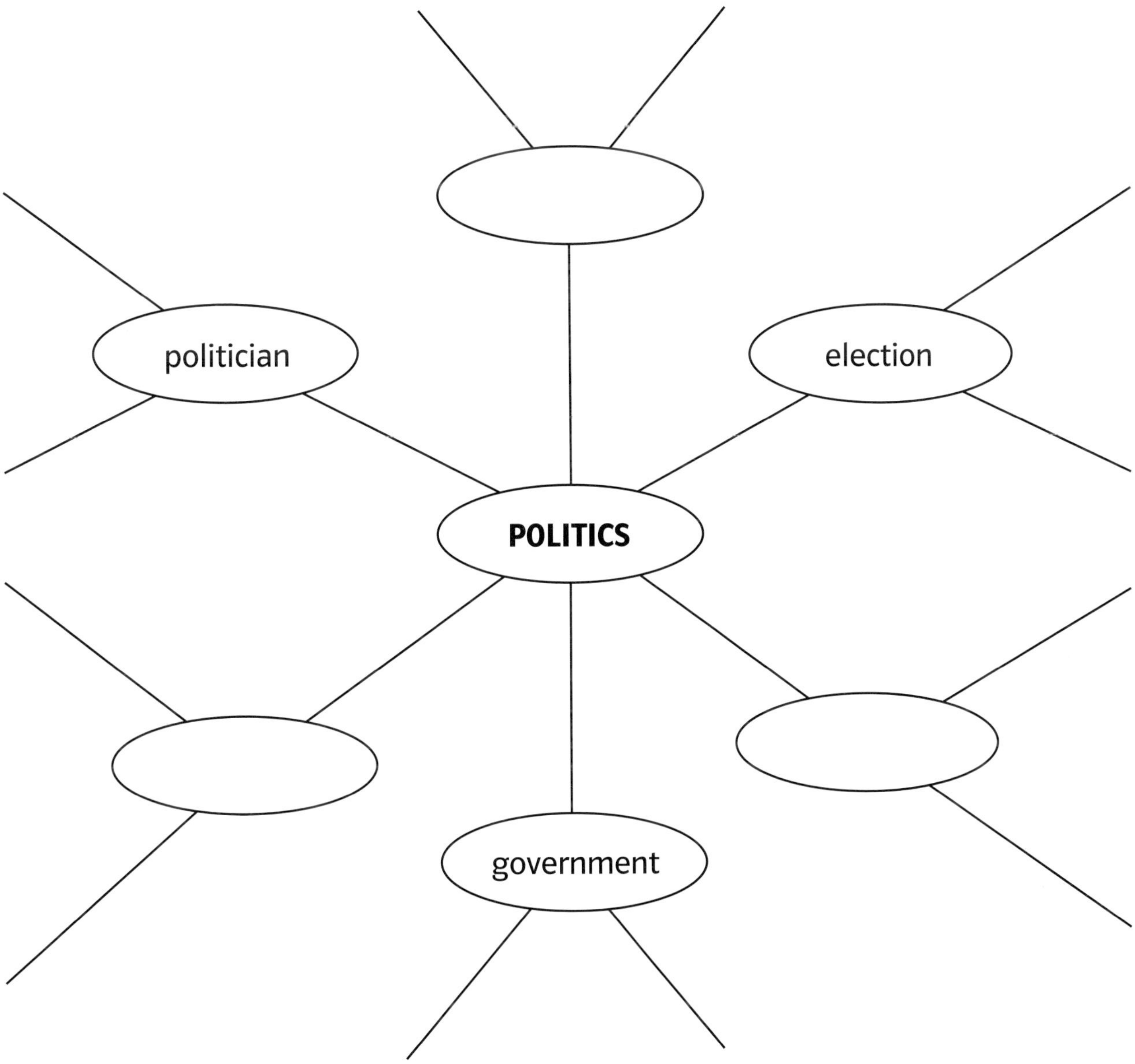
politician
election
POLITICS
government

From your English teacher

From the travel agent

From your parents

From your partner

From the library

From Andrew

From your dentist

From the garage

From the personnel department

From your boss

From your daughter

From your bank

From:
Your bank
Message:
You left your card in the cash machine.

From:
Your partner
Message:
Wants to go out for dinner this evening.

From:
Your dentist
Message:
You need to make an appointment for an annual check-up.

From:
Travel agent
Message:
The tickets for your holiday have arrived.

From:
The public library
Message:
Your books are two weeks overdue.

From:
The garage
Message:
The repairs to your car will cost about Euros €600.

From:
Your parents
Message:
They will arrive tomorrow at 11 a.m.

From:
Andrew
Message:
Needs help with his new computer. Can you go round this evening?

From :
The personnel department
Message:
They need a recent photo.

From:
The boss
Message:
He/She wants to see you tomorrow morning at 7.30 a.m.

From:
Your daughter
Message:
Wants to spend the night at Sara's house.

From:
Your English teacher
Message:
Class starts an hour earlier this week.

The hotel we're	staying in is very expensive.
The guided tour	we took in London was not very interesting.
The most exciting	thing I've ever tried is bungee jumping.
That MP3 player she	bought at the duty free shop doesn't work.
The pictures we looked	at in the museum were all very modern.
The cruise	he took last year went to the Caribbean.
The person you	should talk to is the director.
New York is a city that	never sleeps.
That's the man	who helped us out yesterday.
The opera	I went to last night was excellent.

